Working with a Samsung Galaxy Tablet with Android 5 for SENIORS

Studio Visual Steps

Working with a Samsung Galaxy Tablet with Android 5 for SENIORS

Get started quickly with this user-friendly tablet

www.visualsteps.com

This book has been written using the Visual Steps™ method.
Cover design by Studio Willemien Haagsma bNO

© 2016 Visual Steps
Author: Studio Visual Steps

First printing: January 2016
ISBN 978 90 5905 441 7

Do you have any questions or suggestions?
E-mail: info@visualsteps.com

Would you like more information?
www.visualsteps.com

Website for this book:
www.visualsteps.com/samsungandroid5

Subscribe to the free Visual Steps Newsletter:
www.visualsteps.com/newsletter

Table of Contents

Foreword   11
Introduction to Visual Steps™   12
Visual Steps Newsletter   12
What You Will Need   13
The Website Accompanying This Book   13
How to Use This Book   14
Test Your Knowledge   15
For Teachers   15
The Screen Shots   16

1. The Samsung Galaxy Tab   17
    1.1 Turning On or Unlocking the Samsung Galaxy Tab   18
    1.2 Setting Up the Samsung Galaxy Tab   19
    1.3 The Main Components of the Samsung Galaxy Tab   24
    1.4 Basic Operations on a Samsung Galaxy Tab   29
    1.5 Working with the Onscreen Keyboard   34
    1.6 Automatically Updating the Samsung Galaxy Tab   39
    1.7 Connect to the Internet through Wi-Fi   41
    1.8 Connect to the Internet through a Mobile Data Network   44
    1.9 Downloading and Installing Smart Switch   47
    1.10 Connecting the Samsung Galaxy Tab to the Computer 49
    1.11 Safely Disconnecting the Samsung Galaxy Tab   51
    1.12 Creating and Adding a Google account   52
    1.13 Locking or Turning Off the Samsung Galaxy Tab   57
1.14 Background Information   59
1.15 Tips   63

2. Using Email on Your Tablet   77
    2.1 Opening Email and Adding an Email account   78
    2.2 Sending an Email   81
    2.3 Receiving an Email   85
    2.4 Deleting an Email   87
2.5 Background Information   90
2.6 Tips   91

3. Surfing with Your Tablet   **101**
3.1 Opening the *Internet* app   102
3.2 Opening a Web Page   103
3.3 Zooming In and Out   104
3.4 Scrolling   107
3.5 Opening a Link on a Web Page   109
3.6 Opening a Link in a New Tab   110
3.7 Go to a Previous or Next Page   112
3.8 Adding a Bookmark   113
3.9 Searching   115
3.10 Switching between Recently Used Apps   117
3.11 Background Information   121
3.12 Tips   122

4. Managing Your Contacts, Calendar, and Widgets   **127**
4.1 Adding a Contact   128
4.2 Editing a Contact   134
4.3 Finding a Contact   135
4.4 Deleting a Contact   135
4.5 *S Planner*   136
4.6 Adding an Event to the Calendar   137
4.7 Editing or Deleting an Event   140
4.8 Working with Widgets   142
4.9 Background Information   148
4.10 Tips   149

5. Maps, Google Search, and Managing Files   **157**
5.1 *Maps*   158
5.2 Searching for a Location with *Street View*   161
5.3 Getting Directions   164
5.4 Searching   167
5.5 The *My Files* App   169
5.6 Closing Apps   173
5.7 Background Information   175
5.8 Tips   176

6. Downloading Apps   **185**
6.1 Downloading a Free App   186
6.2 Downloading a Purchased App   190
6.3 Managing Apps   196
6.4 Deleting an App   203
6.5 Background Information   205
6.6 Tips   206

7. Photos and Video   **219**
7.1 Taking Pictures   220
7.2 Filming   222
7.3 Viewing Photos in the *Gallery*   224
7.4 Sending a Photo by Email   228
7.5 Printing a Photo   230
7.6 Copying Photos and Videos to the Computer   232
7.7 Play a Recorded Video   234
7.8 Background Information   236
7.9 Tips   237

8. Music   **245**
8.1 Copying Music to Your Samsung Galaxy Tab   246
8.2 Playing Music   248
8.3 Visual Steps Website and Newsletter   252
8.4 Background Information   253
8.5 Tips   254

Appendices
A. How Do I Do That Again?   **259**
B. Index   **265**

Foreword

Dear readers,

The Samsung Galaxy Tabs are user-friendly, portable multimedia devices that offer a wide range of possibilities. They are suitable for many different purposes. For instance, sending and receiving email messages, surfing the Internet, taking notes, planning a trip, or keeping a calendar.
The Samsung Galaxy Tabs come equipped with a large number of standards apps (programs) that you can use for instance, to work with photos, videos and music. You can also easily share your photos with others.

Apart from that, you can search the *Play Store* for many more free and paid apps. What about games, puzzles, newspapers, magazines, fitness exercises, and photo editing apps? You can find apps for almost any purpose you can think of.

In this book you will learn to use the main options and functions of this versatile tablet.

We hope you have a lot of fun learning how to work with the Samsung Galaxy Tablet!

Studio Visual Steps

PS
We welcome your comments and suggestions regarding this book.
Our email address is: mail@visualsteps.com

Introduction to Visual Steps™

The Visual Steps handbooks and manuals are the best instructional materials available for learning how to work with mobile devices, computers and software applications. Nowhere else will you find better support to help you get started with *Windows*, *Mac OS X*, an iPad or other tablet, an iPhone, the Internet or various software applications such as *Picasa*.

Properties of the Visual Steps books:
- **Comprehensible contents**
  Addresses the needs of the beginner or intermediate user for a manual written in simple, straight-forward English.
- **Clear structure**
  Precise, easy to follow instructions. The material is broken down into small enough segments to allow for easy absorption.
- **Screen shots of every step**
  Quickly compare what you see on your screen with the screen shots in the book. Pointers and tips guide you when new windows, screens or alert boxes are opened so you always know what to do next.
- **Get started right away**
  All you have to do is have your tablet or computer and your book at hand. Sit somewhere comfortable, begin reading and perform the operations as indicated on your own device.
- **Layout**
  The text is printed in a large size font and is clearly legible.

In short, I believe these manuals will be excellent guides for you.

Dr. H. van der Meij
Faculty of Applied Education, Department of Instructional Technology, University of Twente, the Netherlands

Visual Steps Newsletter

All Visual Steps books follow the same methodology: clear and concise step-by-step instructions with screen shots to demonstrate each task.
A complete list of all our books can be found on our website **www.visualsteps.com**
You can also sign up to receive our **free Visual Steps Newsletter**.
In this Newsletter you will receive periodic information by email regarding:
- the latest titles and previously released books;
- special offers, supplemental chapters, tips and free informative booklets.

Also, our Newsletter subscribers may download any of the documents listed on the web page **www.visualsteps.com/info_downloads**
When you subscribe to our Newsletter you can be assured that we will never use your email address for any purpose other than sending you the information as previously described. We will not share this address with any third-party. Each Newsletter also contains a one-click link to unsubscribe.

What You Will Need

To be able to work through this book, you will need a number of things:

A Samsung Galaxy Tablet with *Android 5*.

The screen shots in this book have been made with a Tab 4. You might see slightly different screens if you are working with a different tablet with *Android 5*. The basic operations will remain the same. Big differences will be explained in the relevant sections.

A computer or laptop with the *Smart Switch* program installed. In *section 1.8 Downloading and Installing Smart Switch* you can read how to install *Smart Switch*.
If you do not own a computer or laptop, perhaps you can use a computer owned by a friend or family member to perform certain tasks such as upgrading firmware.

For the printing exercises you will need to have a printer manufactured by Samsung. If you do not own a Samsung printer you can just skip the printing exercises.

The Website Accompanying This Book

On the website that accompanies this book,
www.visualsteps.com/samsungandroid5, you will find more information about the book. This website will also keep you informed of changes you need to know as a user of the book. Be sure to visit our website **www.visualsteps.com** from time to time to read about new books and gather other useful information.

How to Use This Book

This book has been written using the Visual Steps™ method. The method is simple: you put the book next to your Samsung Galaxy Tab and perform each task step by step, directly on your device. With the clear instructions and the multitude of screen shots, you will always know exactly what to do next. By working through all the tasks in each chapter, you will gain a full understanding of your Samsung Galaxy Tab. You can also skip a chapter and go to one that suits your needs.

In this Visual Steps™ book, you will see various icons. This is what they mean:

Techniques
These icons indicate an action to be carried out:

 The index finger indicates you need to do something on the Tab's screen, for instance, tap something or type a text.

 The keyboard icon means you should type something on the keyboard of your Samsung Galaxy Tab or your computer.

 The mouse icon means you need to do something with the mouse on your computer.

 The hand icon means you should do something else, for example rotate the Tab or turn it off. It can also point to a task previously learned.

In some areas of this book additional icons indicate warnings or helpful hints. These help you to avoid making mistakes and alert you when a decision needs to be made.

Help
These icons indicate that extra help is available:

 The arrow icon warns you about something.

 The bandage icon will help you if something has gone wrong.

 Have you forgotten how to do something? The number next to the footsteps tells you where to look it up at the end of the book in the appendix *How Do I Do That Again?*

In separate boxes you will find general information or tips concerning the Tab.

Extra information
Information boxes are denoted by these icons:

 The book icon gives you extra background information that you can read at your convenience. This extra information is not necessary for working through the book.

 The light bulb icon indicates an extra tip for using the Samsung Galaxy Tab.

Test Your Knowledge

After you have worked through this book, you can test your knowledge online, at the **www.ccforseniors.com** website. By answering a number of multiple choice questions you will be able to test your knowledge. After you have finished the test, you will receive a *Computer Certificate*. Participating in the test is **free of charge**. The computer certificate website is a free Visual Steps service.

For Teachers

The Visual Steps books have been written as self-study guides for individual use. They are also well suited for use in a group or classroom setting. For this purpose, some of our books come with a free teacher's manual. You can download the available teacher's manuals and additional materials from the website: **www.visualsteps.com/instructor**

The Screen Shots

The screen shots in this book indicate which button, file or hyperlink you need to click on your computer or tablet screen. In the instruction text (in **bold** letters) you will see a small image of the item you need to tap or click. The line will point you to the right place on your screen.

The small screen shots that are printed in this book are not meant to be completely legible all the time. This is not necessary, as you will see these images on your own tablet screen, in real size and fully legible.

Here you see an example of such an instruction text and a screen shot of the item you need to click. The line indicates where to find this item on your own screen:

Sometimes the screen shot shows only a portion of a window. Here is an example:

We would like to emphasize that we **do not intend you** to read the information in all of the screen shots in this book. Always use the screen shots in combination with the display on your Samsung Galaxy Tab screen.

1. The Samsung Galaxy Tablet

The Samsung Galaxy Tab is an easy-to-use tablet made by Samsung which will enable you to do many things. Not only can you surf the Internet and send emails, you can also keep a calendar, play games, take pictures, shoot videos and read books, papers or magazines. All these things are done by using *apps*. Apps are the programs installed on the Samsung Galaxy Tab. Along with the standard apps that are already installed on your tablet; you can add many (free and paid) apps by using the *Play Store*. This is the web shop where you can acquire new apps.

If you connect your Samsung Galaxy Tab to the computer you can use the free *Smart Switch* program to manage the content of your tablet. After you have safely disconnected the tablet from the computer, you can use the tablet anywhere you want. Depending on the type of tablet you have purchased, you can connect to the Internet through a wireless network (Wi-Fi), or through a mobile data network.

In this chapter you will become acquainted with the Samsung Galaxy Tab and you will learn the basic operations for using the tablet and the onscreen keyboard.

In this chapter you will learn how to:

- turn on or unlock the Samsung Galaxy Tab;
- set up the Samsung Galaxy Tab;
- use the main components of the Samsung Galaxy Tab;
- perform basic operations on the Samsung Galaxy Tab;
- work with the onscreen keyboard;
- update the Samsung Galaxy Tab;
- connect to the Internet through a wireless network (Wi-Fi);
- connect to the Internet through a mobile data network;
- download and install *Smart Switch*;
- connect the Samsung Galaxy Tab to the computer;
- safely disconnect the Samsung Galaxy Tab;
- create a *Google* account;
- register your *Google* account on your tablet;
- lock or turn off the Samsung Galaxy Tab.

Please note:

If you are working with a Samsung Tab with Android 5 other than a Tab 4, the screens you see on your Tab may look slightly different from the images in this book. The buttons may also have a different name and/or look a little different. Always try to find a similar button or function. The basic operations will remain the same.

1.1 Turning On or Unlocking the Samsung Galaxy Tab

The Samsung Galaxy Tab may be turned off or locked. If your Tab is turned off, you can turn it on by pressing and holding the Power/Lock button. This button is located on the upper of right-hand side of the tablet:

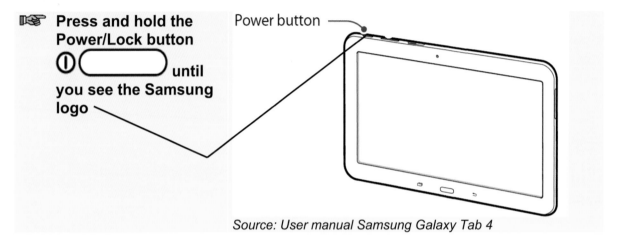

☞ **Press and hold the Power/Lock button** until **you see the Samsung logo**

Power button

Source: User manual Samsung Galaxy Tab 4

Or:

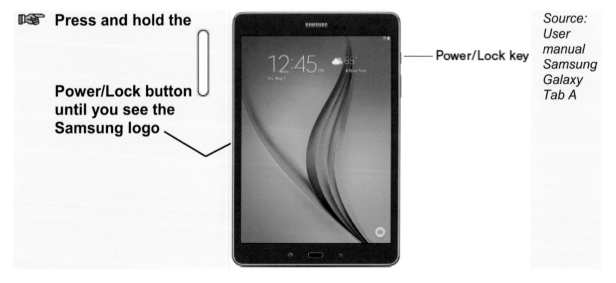

☞ **Press and hold the**

Power/Lock button until you see the Samsung logo

Power/Lock key

Source: User manual Samsung Galaxy Tab A

The Tab is turned on.

Your Tab may be locked. The screen will be dark and does not react to touch gestures. If this is the case, you can unlock the Tab like this:

 **Briefly press the Power/Lock button**

You may still need to unlock the screen as well:

☞ **Place your fingers somewhere on the right-hand side of the screen**

☞ **Drag across the right-hand side of the screen**

If this is the first time you turn on the Samsung Galaxy Tab, you will see a few screens where you can enter various settings. In the next section you can read how to do this. If you have previously used your Samsung Galaxy Tab, you can continue with *section 1.3 The Main Components of the Samsung Galaxy Tab* on page 24.

1.2 Setting Up the Samsung Galaxy Tab

You can set the language for the Samsung Galaxy Tab:

If English (United States) has already been selected:

☞ **Tap** START ❯

You might see another button. In that case, instead of START ❯ you need to

tap → on your tablet.

If another language has been selected:

☞ **Tap the language**

☞ **Tap** English (United States)

☞ **Tap** START ❯

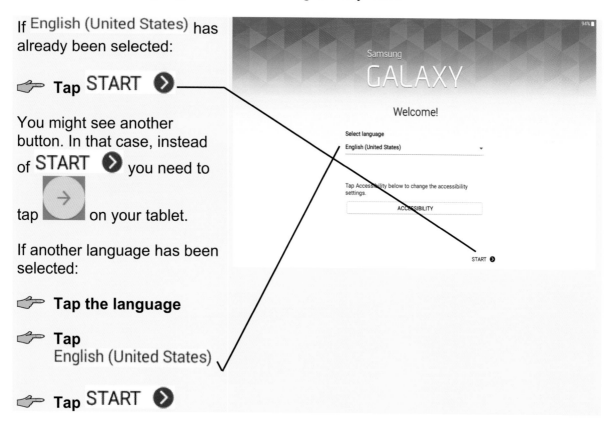

 **Please note:**

Please note that the screen is hold in the horizontal (landscape) position.

On the next screen you may see a message regarding a SIM card:

 **If necessary, tap SKIP ❯**

On the next screen you can set up a Wi-Fi connection. You can skip this step for now:

At the bottom of the window:

Tap NEXT ❯

In the next screen you will be asked to agree to the licensing agreement, and whether you want to send any error log messages in case the update procedure on the Tab does not work:

Tap a checkmark ✓ by I understand and agree

If necessary, tap the radio button ⦿ by Yes

Tap NEXT ❯

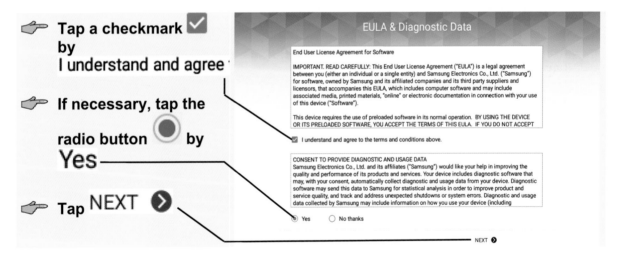

If you are working with a different Samsung tablet your screen might look like this:

☞ **Tap a checkmark** ☑ **by**
CONSENT TO PROVIDE

☞ **Tap NEXT >**

A small window appears:

☞ **Tap AGREE**

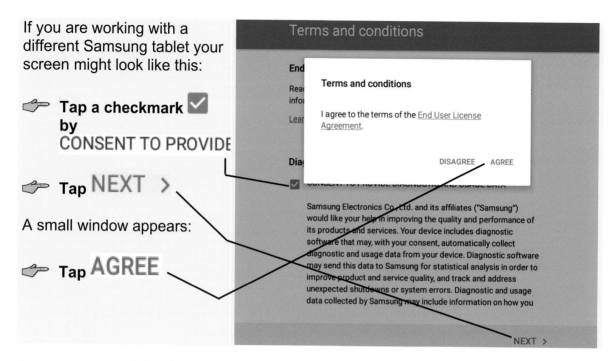

Now you can set the date and time:

If the time zone and the time are not yet correct:

☞ **Tap** ▼

☞ **Drag upwards across the screen until you see your time zone**

☞ **Tap your time zone, for example**
Eastern Standard Time
GMT-05:00

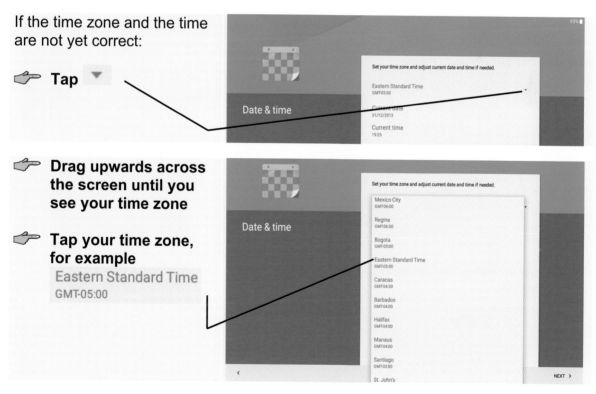

Now the time zone is correct:

☞ **Tap NEXT >**

In the screen that is displayed you can enter the name of the tablet's owner:

⌨ **Type your first name, if you wish** ————

☞ **Tap NEXT**

⌨ **Type your last name, if you wish** ———

☞ **Tap Done** ————

☞ **Tap NEXT** ➤

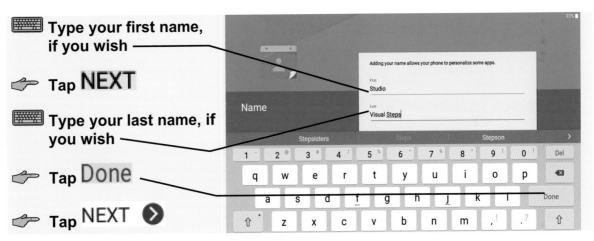

In the next screen you will be asked whether you want to use the *Google location services*. This service uses information from a Wi-Fi or mobile data network to determine your location, even when you are not using your tablet. This information is used to enhance *Google* search results, among other things.

If you wish, you can uncheck the boxes:

☞ **If you wish, tap the boxes ☑** ———

When you see ☐ the option is not active anymore.

☞ **Tap NEXT ›**

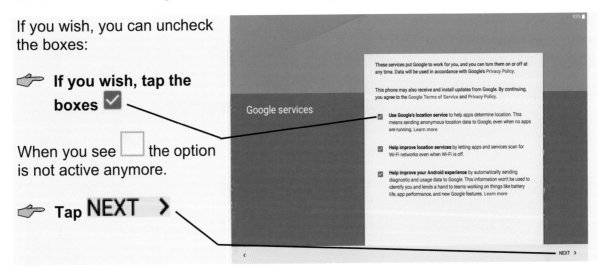

In the next screen you can set up a Samsung account. You can skip this step for the time being:

☞ **Tap SKIP** ➤

Now you will be asked if you are sure.

☞ **Tap SKIP**

You might see one more screen, regarding the *Dropbox* storage service. You can skip this screen:

 **Tap** SKIP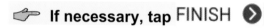

Now the device is set up and ready for use:

 **If necessary, tap** FINISH ❯

↘ Please note:

While you are using your tablet you may see some screens that provide information about the operation of an app or the keyboard. You can read the information and tap OK afterwards.

You may see a window on the right-hand side. This window will disappear by itself:

You will see the home screen:

Please note that the screen is hold in the horizontal (landscape) position.

If you are working with a different Samsung tablet, the home screen might look like this:

HELP! My Samsung Galaxy Tab is locked.

If you do not use the Samsung Galaxy Tab for a while, it will automatically lock. The default setting for locking is after 30 seconds of inactivity. This is how you unlock the Samsung Galaxy Tab:

☞ **Briefly press the Power/Lock button**

☞ **Place your fingers somewhere on the screen**

☞ **Drag across the screen**

1.3 The Main Components of the Samsung Galaxy Tab

In the images below you see the main components of most Samsung Galaxy Tablets. When an operation regarding a specific component is described, you can return here to find the relevant component in these images.

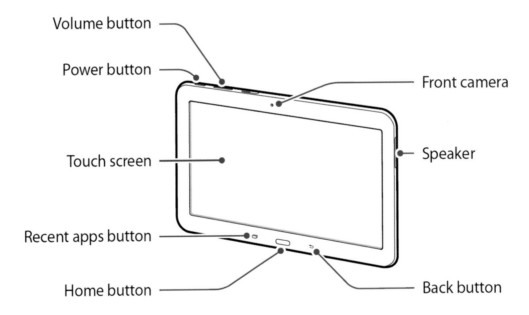

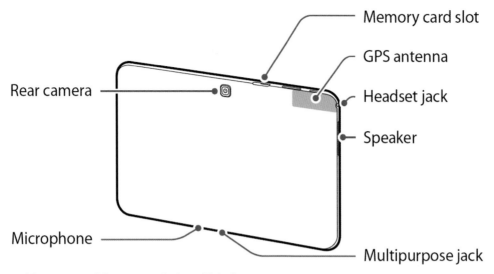

Memory card slot

GPS antenna

Rear camera

Headset jack

Speaker

Microphone

Multipurpose jack

Source: User manual Samsung Galaxy Tab 4

On some type of tablets, the memory card slot and the multipurpose jack can be found on the right-hand side.

It is also possible the components of your tablet are located like this:

Proximity and gesture sensors

Front camera

Power/Lock key

Volume key

Recent apps

Back

Home key

Microphone — Rear camera

SAMSUNG

MicroSD card slot —

Speaker —   — Speaker

USB charger/
Accessory port   — Headset jack

Source: User manual Samsung Galaxy Tab A

On the home screen you will immediately notice the large rectangular panels. Most Samsung tablets have two of these panels. These panels are actually *widgets,* small applications that provide information and useful functions:

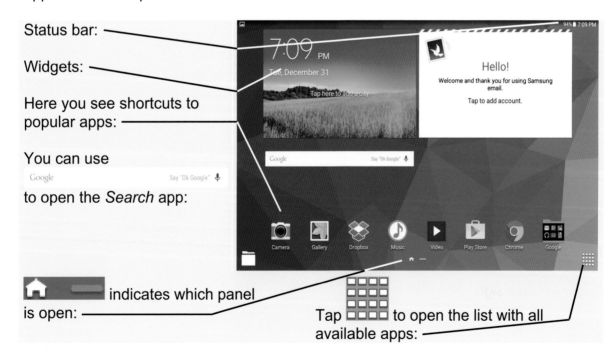

Status bar: —

Widgets: —

Here you see shortcuts to popular apps: —

You can use

Google   Say "Ok Google"

to open the *Search* app:

🏠 ▭   indicates which panel is open: —

Tap ▦ to open the list with all available apps: —

Here you see another home screen:

Status bar:

Widget:

Here you see shortcuts to
popular apps:

You can use

Google

to open the *Search* app:

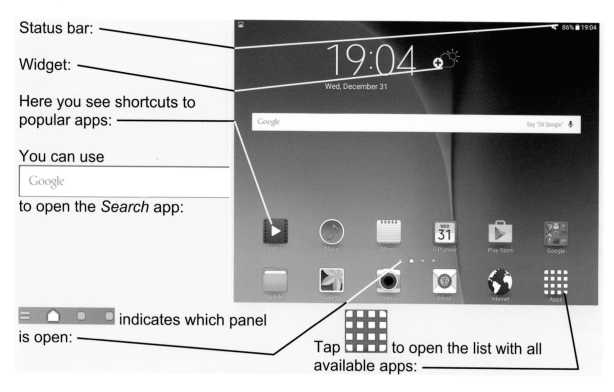

indicates which panel
is open:

Tap ⬚⬚⬚ to open the list with all
available apps:

At the top of the screen you see the status bar. The current time is displayed on the
status bar. To the left of the time indicator, you will see small icons that provide
information regarding the status of the Tab and its connections. Below you see a list
of possible icons that you may see and what they indicate:

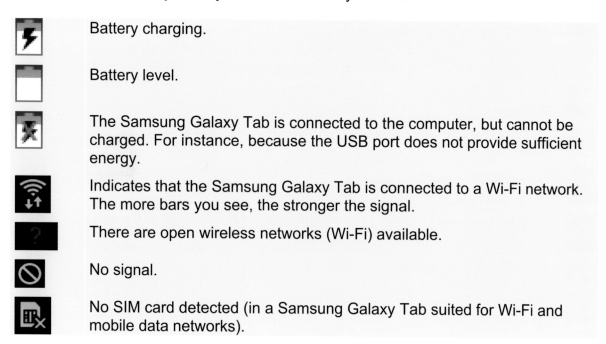

Battery charging.

Battery level.

The Samsung Galaxy Tab is connected to the computer, but cannot be
charged. For instance, because the USB port does not provide sufficient
energy.

Indicates that the Samsung Galaxy Tab is connected to a Wi-Fi network.
The more bars you see, the stronger the signal.

There are open wireless networks (Wi-Fi) available.

No signal.

No SIM card detected (in a Samsung Galaxy Tab suited for Wi-Fi and
mobile data networks).

Indicates that the Samsung Galaxy Tab with Wi-Fi + 3G/4G is not connected to a mobile data network.

 Indicates that your provider's 3G or 4G network (on the Samsung Galaxy Tab Wi-Fi + 3G/4G) is available and that you can connect to the Internet through 3G or 4G.

 Indicates that your provider's EDGE network (on the Samsung Galaxy Tab Wi-Fi + 3G/4G models) is available and that you can connect to the Internet through EDGE.

 Indicates that your provider's GPRS network (on the Samsung Galaxy Tab Wi-Fi + 3G/4G models) is available and that you can connect to the Internet through GPRS.

 Active call (on Samsung Galaxy Tab Wi-Fi + 3G/4G models).

 Call waiting (on Samsung Galaxy Tab Wi-Fi + 3G/4G models).

 Missed call (on Samsung Galaxy Tab Wi-Fi + 3G/4G models).

 Call forwarding has been activated (on Samsung Galaxy Tab Wi-Fi + 3G/4G models).

 Smart stay has been enabled.

 Bluetooth has been enabled.

 Airplane mode has been enabled. When your Samsung Galaxy Tab is in this mode, you will not have Internet access, and you will not be able to use any Bluetooth devices. Nor will you be able to make any calls or send text messages, if you have a Samsung Galaxy Tab Wi-Fi + 3G/4G model.

 Music playback.

 Warning: an error has occurred, or you need to be cautious.

 Connected to the computer.

 Message notification. This may indicate that an update is available, for example.

 Screen print has been made.

 Alarm is set.

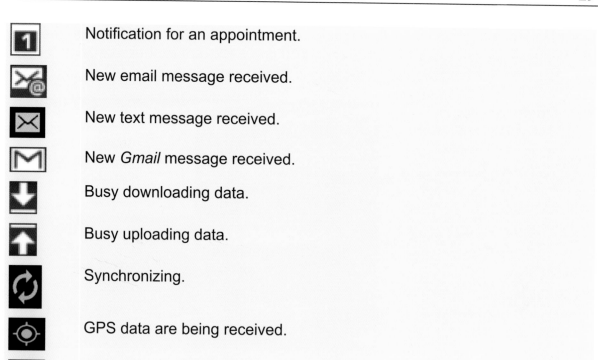

Notification for an appointment.

New email message received.

New text message received.

New *Gmail* message received.

Busy downloading data.

Busy uploading data.

Synchronizing.

GPS data are being received.

Options for opening the onscreen keyboard.

1.4 Basic Operations on a Samsung Galaxy Tab

The Samsung Galaxy Tab is very easy to use. In this section you will be practicing some basic operations and touch gestures:

☞ **If necessary, briefly press the Power/Lock button**

If you see a screen like this, you will need to unlock the Tab first:

☞ **Drag your finger across the screen**

Your screen might look a bit different.

Now you see the home screen. Although you have set the date and time with the set up, the date and time may not be correct. You can easily adjust these settings. First, you open the *Notification Panel*:

☞ **Drag your finger downwards, starting at the top of the screen**

You will see the *Notification Panel*. In this window you can view messages concerning the status of the Samsung Galaxy Tab, and you can change a few settings. In the *Settings* app you can change many more settings:

☞ **Tap** ⚙

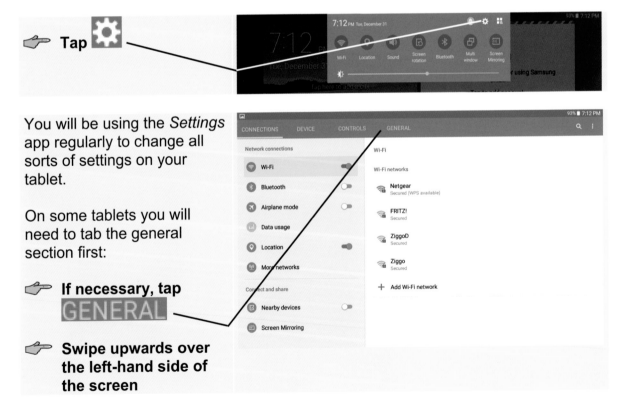

You will be using the *Settings* app regularly to change all sorts of settings on your tablet.

On some tablets you will need to tab the general section first:

☞ **If necessary, tap** GENERAL

☞ **Swipe upwards over the left-hand side of the screen**

☞ **Tap**

🗓 Date and time

☞ **Uncheck the box ☑ by**
Automatic date and t

You might see 🔘 on your screen. In that case tap 🔘.

☞ **Tap** Set date

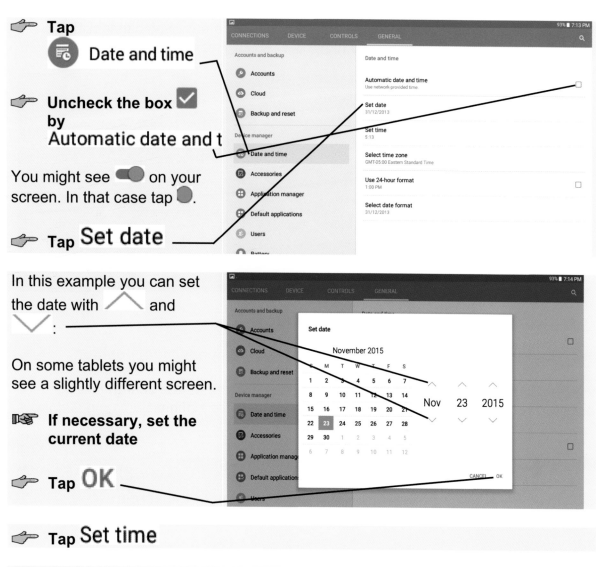

In this example you can set the date with ⋀ and ⋁ :

On some tablets you might see a slightly different screen.

☞ **If necessary, set the current date**

☞ **Tap** OK

☞ **Tap** Set time

☞ **If necessary, set the time**

☞ **Tap** OK

The default setting for the screen of the Samsung Galaxy Tab is that it rotates as you turn the device. Just try it:

☞ **Hold the Samsung Galaxy Tab in an upright position**

Now you will see that the image is displayed in portrait mode. You can lock the screen, so it will not rotate when you move the tablet. You do that like this:

☞ **Drag your finger downwards, starting at the top of the screen**

You will see the *Notification Panel:*

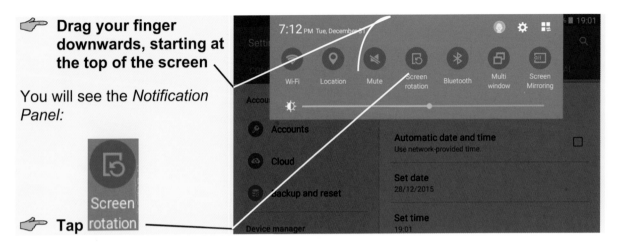

☞ **Tap** Screen rotation

You can check to see if the new setting works:

☞ **Hold the Samsung Galaxy Tab in a horizontal (landscape) position**

Now you will see that the image on the Tab does not rotate. The screen has been locked in portrait mode. If you do want to rotate the screen of the Samsung Galaxy Tab when you turn the device, you can do this:

☞ **Hold the Samsung Galaxy Tab in an upright position**

☞ **Drag your finger downwards, starting at the top of the screen**

☞ **Tap** Screen rotation

Now the screen will rotate as you turn the tablet to a different position.

☞ **Hold the Samsung Galaxy Tab in a horizontal (landscape) position**

The image on the tablet is displayed in landscape mode.

The *Accessibility* section contains more options than can be displayed on the screen. Now open the *Accessibility* section:

☞ **If necessary, tap**
DEVICE

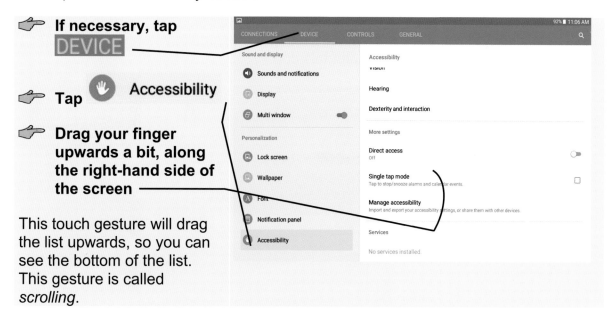

☞ **Tap ✋ Accessibility**

☞ **Drag your finger upwards a bit, along the right-hand side of the screen**

This touch gesture will drag the list upwards, so you can see the bottom of the list. This gesture is called *scrolling*.

You can also do this the other way round:

☞ **Drag your finger downwards, along the right-hand side of the screen**

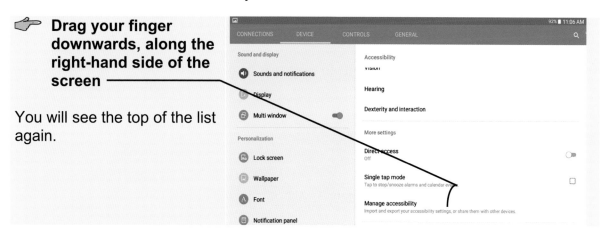

You will see the top of the list again.

Now you can leave the *Settings* app and go back to the home screen. For this you can use the Home button on your tablet:

🖙 **Press the Home button**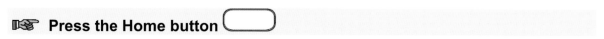

➴ **Please note:**
The screen shots for this book were made holding the tablet in a horizontal (landscape) position. We recommend you also hold the tablet in a horizontal position as you perform the operations described in this book. Otherwise, the screens on your tablet will look slightly different from the images in this book.

1.5 Working with the Onscreen Keyboard

Your Samsung Galaxy Tab is equipped with a useful onscreen keyboard that is displayed whenever you need to type something. For example, when you take notes in the *Memo* app. Here is how you open this app:

You will see the apps installed on your tablet. This is how you open the *Memo* app:

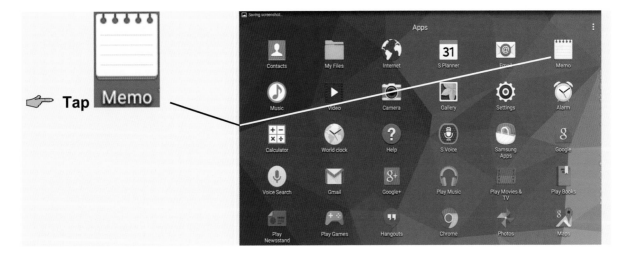

 Please note:
While you are working with your Tab, you may see screens that provide additional information regarding the use of an app. You can read this information and tap OK afterwards.

Open a new, blank memo page:

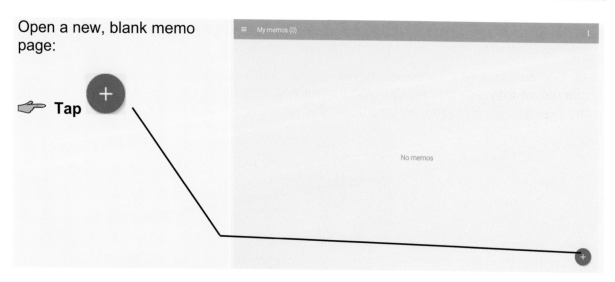

 Tap

The onscreen keyboard works just like a regular keyboard. Only, you need to tap the keys instead of pressing them. Just try it:

Type:
  This is a test.

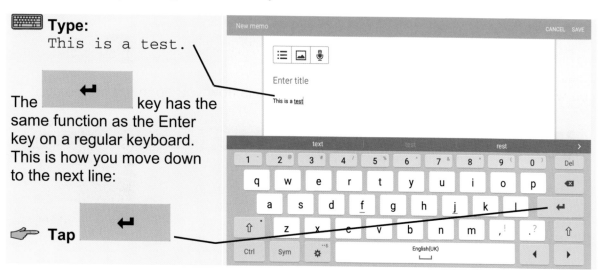

The ⏎ key has the same function as the Enter key on a regular keyboard. This is how you move down to the next line:

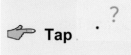 **Tap**

Tip

Comma, period, exclamation mark, question mark
The comma and the exclamation mark share a key on the Tab's onscreen keyboard, just like the period and the question mark. This is how you type the lowest symbol on a key, for instance, a period:

Tap

- Continue on the next page -

And this is how you type the uppermost symbol on a key, the question mark, for instance:

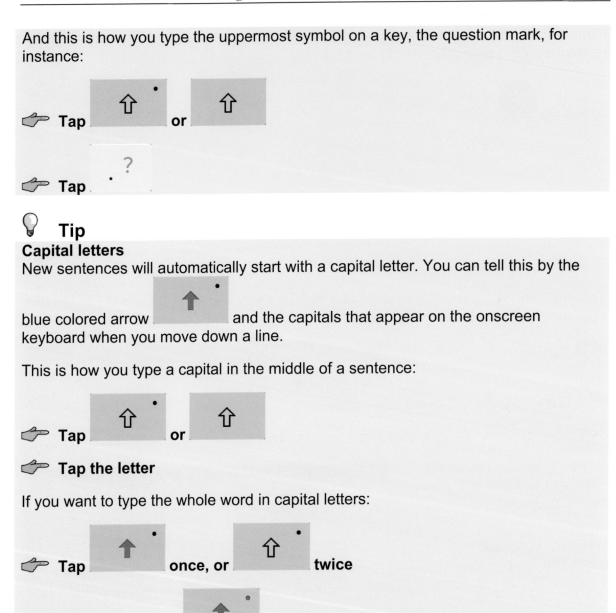

☞ Tap ⇧ or ⇧

☞ Tap ?

💡 **Tip**

Capital letters
New sentences will automatically start with a capital letter. You can tell this by the blue colored arrow ⬆ and the capitals that appear on the onscreen keyboard when you move down a line.

This is how you type a capital in the middle of a sentence:

☞ Tap ⇧ or ⇧

☞ **Tap the letter**

If you want to type the whole word in capital letters:

☞ Tap ⬆ once, or ⇧ twice

If the key looks like this ⬆, everything will be displayed in capitals.

Type the beginning of a simple sum:

⌨ **Type:** 12

In the default keyboard view, you will not see any special symbols. If you want to type the minus sign, you can use a different view:

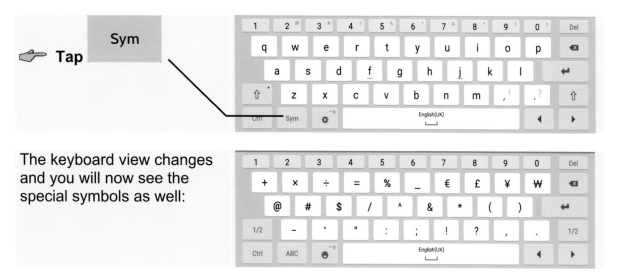

The keyboard view changes and you will now see the special symbols as well:

Type the remainder of the sum:

 **Type:** `-10=3`

If you have typed the wrong character, you can correct this with the Backspace key:

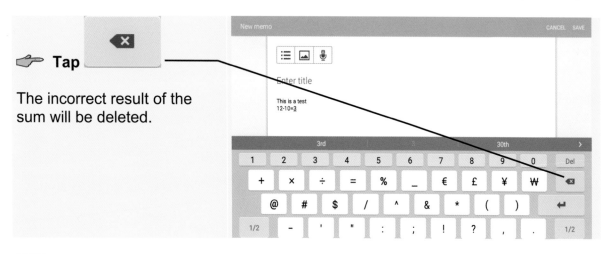

The incorrect result of the sum will be deleted.

 **Type:** 2

Now the result is correct.

💡 Tip

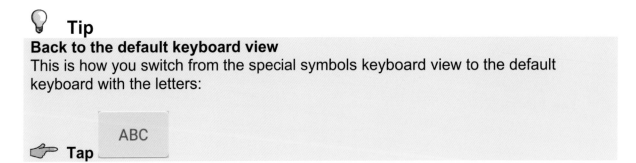

Back to the default keyboard view
This is how you switch from the special symbols keyboard view to the default keyboard with the letters:

☞ **Tap** ABC

This is how you save the memo:

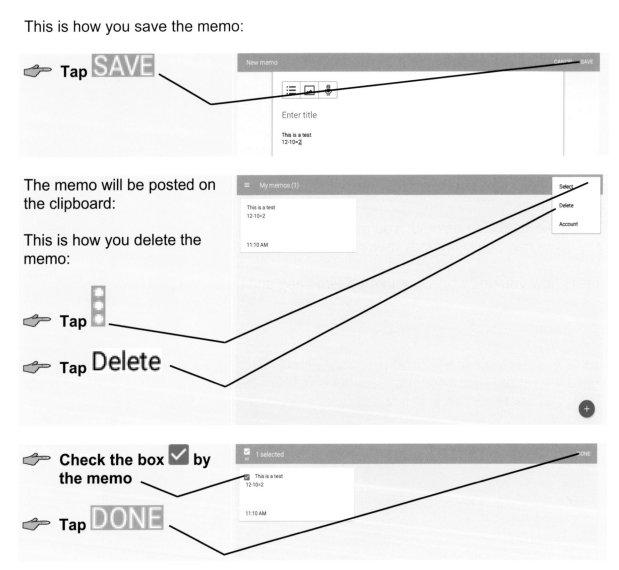

☞ **Tap** SAVE

The memo will be posted on the clipboard:

This is how you delete the memo:

☞ **Tap** ⋮

☞ **Tap** Delete

☞ **Check the box** ✓ **by the memo**

☞ **Tap** DONE

If you are working on a different tablet you can delete the memo like this:

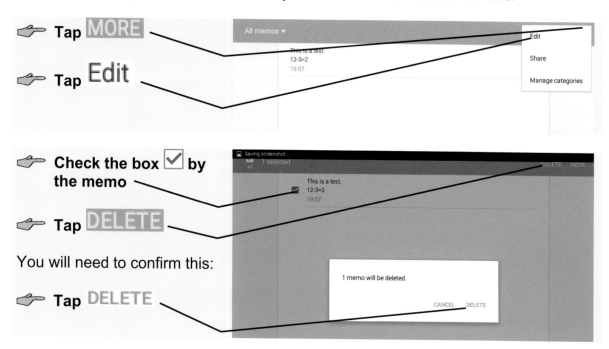

☞ **Tap** MORE

☞ **Tap** Edit

☞ **Check the box** ☑ **by the memo**

☞ **Tap** DELETE

You will need to confirm this:

☞ **Tap** DELETE

The memo has been deleted. You might see a message at the bottom of the screen where you can see how many memos you have deleted.

This is how you quit working with the *Memo* app and go back to the home screen:

☞ **Press the Home button** ⬭

At this point you have practiced using some basic operations and touch gestures. There are other touch gestures, such as scrolling sideways, and zooming in and out. These will be discussed in the chapters where you need to use them.

1.6 Automatically Updating the Samsung Galaxy Tab

Samsung releases regular updates of the Samsung Galaxy Tab software. In these updates, problems are solved, or new functions are added. You can check whether the system automatically searches for software updates. In order to do this, you need to open the *Settings* app again. You can also do this directly from the home screen:

☞ **Tap**  **and** Settings

The *Settings* app may already be placed on the home screen of your Tab.

On some tablets:

☞ **Tap** GENERAL

On all devices:

☞ **Drag upwards along
the left-hand side of
the screen**

☞ **Tap**
ⓘ **About device**

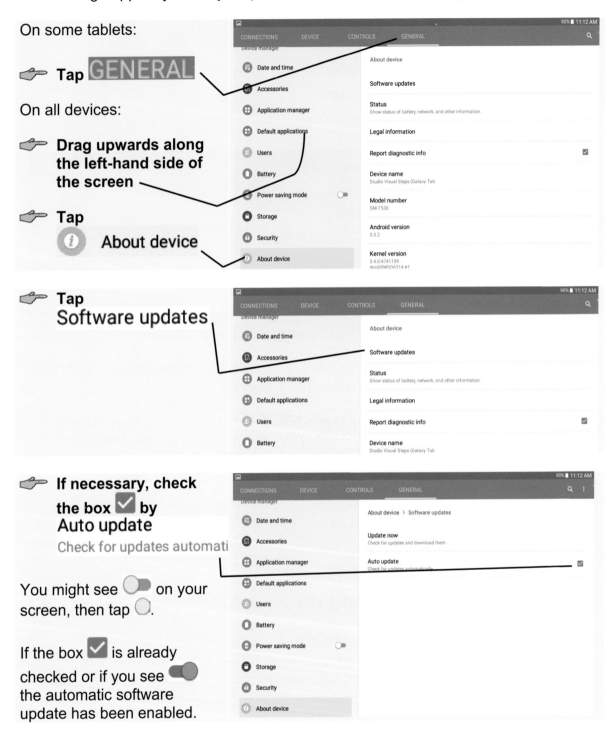

☞ **Tap
Software updates**

☞ **If necessary, check
the box ☑ by
Auto update**
Check for updates automati

You might see 🔘 on your
screen, then tap ⚪.

If the box ☑ is already
checked or if you see 🔘
the automatic software
update has been enabled.

The software update is activated. If a new version of the software is found, it will automatically be installed. Sometimes you will receive a message regarding this action. In that case:

☞ **If necessary, follow the instructions in the screens**

☞ **Press the Home button**

♀ **Tip**
Update through Smart Switch
You can also install an update through *Smart Switch*. In order to do this, first you will need to connect the Samsung Galaxy Tab to the computer. In the *Tips* at the end of this chapter you can read more about this subject.

1.7 Connect to the Internet through Wi-Fi

If you have access to a wireless network, you can connect to the Internet in the following way.

🖐 **Please note:**
If you want to work through this section you will need to have access to a wireless network (Wi-Fi). If you do not have access, you can just read through this section.

Open the *Notification Panel*:

☞ **Drag your finger downwards, starting at the top of the screen**

The *Notification Panel* is displayed. You can connect to a Wi-Fi network like this:

☞ **Place your finger on** **Wi-Fi , and hold it down for a moment**

A window with the available Wi-Fi networks will be opened:

 Tap the network you want to use

Please note: if a Wi-Fi network has already been set up, you will not see this window and the connection will be established right away. On the next page you can read more about this subject.

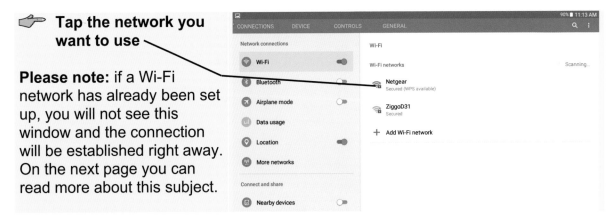

If the network name is indicated as a secure network, such as

Netgear
Secured (WPS available), you will need to enter a password in order to use it.

If necessary, type the password

 If necessary, tap CONNECT

A connection is established with the wireless network:

The symbol on the status bar indicates that there is a connection with a wireless network:

HELP! I do not see the status bar.

The status bar is almost always displayed at once. You may not see the status bar. This is how you display the status bar:

Drag your finger downwards, starting at the top of the screen

In future, a connection with known wireless networks will automatically be established when you turn on Wi-Fi. You can verify this, by turning the Wi-Fi off:

☞ **If necessary, display the status bar** 𝒪𝒪²

☞ **Open the *Notification Panel*** 𝒪𝒪¹

☞ **Tap** Wi-Fi

Now Wi-Fi is turned off, and the button looks like this Wi-Fi . You can re-connect again:

☞ **Tap** Wi-Fi

The connection with the wireless network you have previously used is automatically established. And Wi-Fi is turned on again.

💡 **Tip**

Leave Wi-Fi turned on
It is a good idea to leave the Wi-Fi function turned on. This way, you will be permanently connected to the Internet, and you will receive all relevant updates, email messages, etcetera.

☞ **Press the Home button**

1.8 Connect to the Internet through a Mobile Data Network

If your Samsung Galaxy Tab is also suited for a 3G or 4G mobile data network as well as Wi-Fi, you can also connect to the Internet through this network. A mobile data network is useful when there is no Wi-Fi available. In order to use this network you need to have a SIM card with a data subscription, or a prepaid mobile Internet card. If you do not have a SIM card, you can just read through this section or skip to the following section.

 Tip

Mobile Internet
Since the Samsung Galaxy Tab does not have a simlock, you are free to choose your own mobile Internet service provider. Service providers such as AT&T, Time Warner Cable, and Verizon offer data subscriptions with a SIM card, and most cards are suitable for the Samsung Galaxy Tab, although you always need to check this. Prepaid mobile Internet cards are offered by T-mobile, AT&T, and Ready SIM, among other companies.
The fees and conditions are subject to regular changes. Visit the providers' websites for more information.

Before you can insert the SIM card, you need to turn off the Tab completely:

☞ **Press the Power/Lock button ⓞ▭ until you see this screen**

☞ **Tap** ⏻ **Power off**

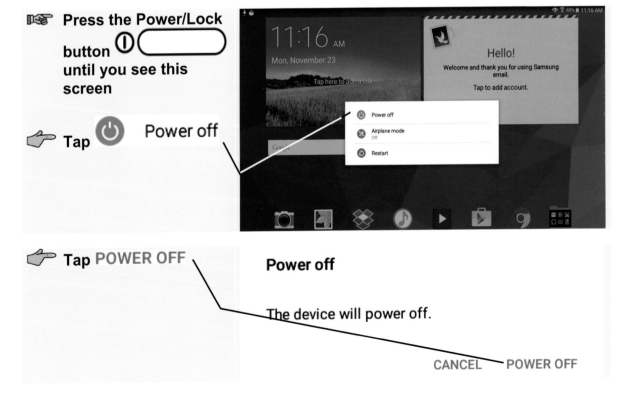

☞ **Tap** POWER OFF

Power off

The device will power off.

CANCEL   POWER OFF

☞ **Open the cover of the SIM card slot**

☞ **Insert the SIM card into the SIM card slot, make sure the gold-colored module is face down**

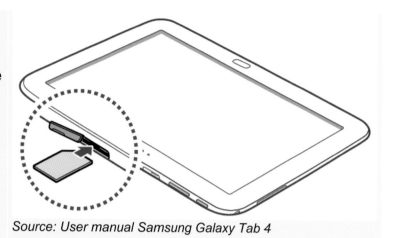

☞ **Press until the SIM card clicks into position**

Be careful not to touch the gold-colored part. This may damage the card.

Source: User manual Samsung Galaxy Tab 4

Please note:

This is what you do if you want to remove the card. First, press the SIM card downwards a little, then the SIM card will be released and move upwards. You will then be able to get hold of the card.

☞ **Close the cover of the SIM card slot**

Now you can turn on the Tab again:

☞ **Turn on the Samsung Galaxy Tab again** 👣4

The system will automatically connect to the mobile data network.

When the connection has been established, you will see the signal strength in the status bar, and the type of mobile data network **4G⬆⬇** that is used:

Please note:

If the connection is not established automatically, you may need to adjust a few more settings. Follow the instructions in the windows. You can also try to find additional information on your service provider's website.

You can temporarily turn off the Internet connection through the mobile data network, if necessary. For example, you can do this if you want to prevent your children (or grandchildren) from using your prepaid credit when they want to play games on your Samsung Galaxy Tab. You can turn off the connection like this:

 **Open the *Notification Panel*** [1]

 **Tap**

You may see a warning about not being able to use certain apps through mobile networks:

☞ **Tap OK**

Now the use of mobile data has been turned off:

The status bar just displays

this symbol 📶 :

This means that you are only connected to a Wi-Fi network.

 Please note:

When you are using mobile data, the **Roaming** function is disabled by default. *Data roaming* means you are using the data network of a different provider, in case your own provider is unavailable. Be careful if you enable this function while abroad. You could incur huge data roaming fees.

Now you can activate the mobile data network again.

 **Open the *Notification Panel*** [1]

☞ **Tap**

☞ **Press the Home button** ⬭

1.9 Downloading and Installing Smart Switch

You can also connect the device to your computer or notebook. With the free *Smart Switch* program, you can create a backup copy and then synchronize the contact information from the *Outlook* program on your computer with your tablet, for example. Synchronizing means equalling the content of your tablet to the content of the data in *Smart Switch*.

First, you need to install *Smart Switch* to your computer or laptop:

☞ **Open the website www.samsung.com/us/smart-switch** 🐾⁶

↪ **Please note:**
If you have already installed *Smart Switch* to your computer, you can continue reading in *section 1.10 Connecting the Samsung Galaxy Tab to the Computer.*

↪ **Please note:**
If you do not have a computer, you can just read through these sections and continue with *section 1.12 Creating and Adding a Google Account.*

👉 **Drag the scroll block downwards**

👉 **Click**

DOWNLOAD FOR PC

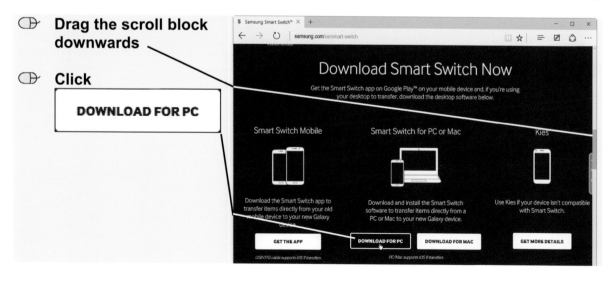

Click   Run

Now your screen may turn dark and you will need to give permission to continue:

☞ If necessary, give permission to continue

By License agreement and Personal Information Collection and Use Agreement:

- Check the box ☑ by I accept the terms of the license agreement

- Click   Next >

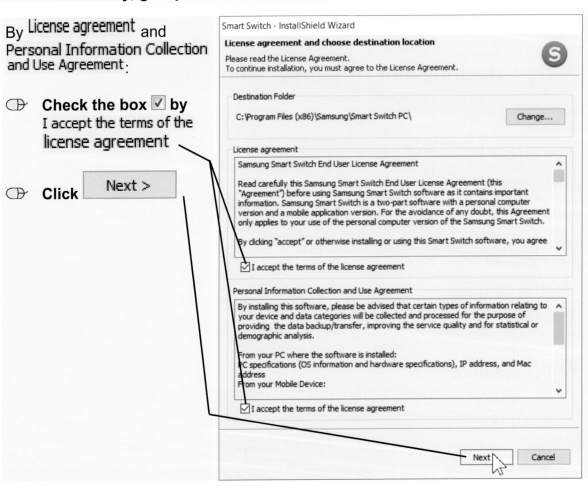

You will see the progress of the installation procedure:

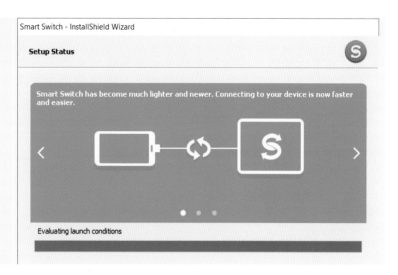

The installation continues. This may take a while.

You do not need to open the program right away:

☞ **If you wish, you can uncheck** ☑ **the boxes by** Create Shortcut on Deskt and Run Smart Switch

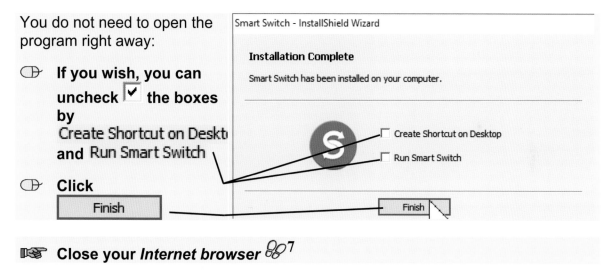

☞ **Click** Finish

☞ **Close your *Internet browser*** ⧉⁷

1.10 Connecting the Samsung Galaxy Tab to the Computer

Before you connect the Samsung Galaxy Tab to the computer, first you need to open *Smart Switch*. In *Windows 10* you start by clicking the search function on the Taskbar:

☞ **Click** 🔍 **or the search box**

On the desktop in *Windows 10* and on the Start screen in *Windows 8.1*:

 **Type:** `Smart Switch`

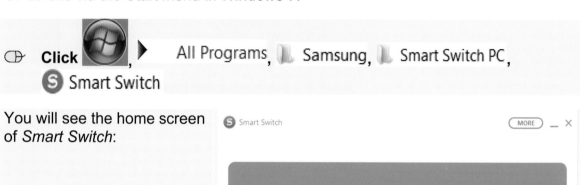

Or do this via the Start menu in *Windows 7*:

You will see the home screen of *Smart Switch*:

Now you can connect the Tab. This is how you do it:

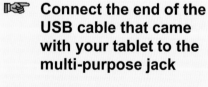 **Connect the end of the USB cable that came with your tablet to the multi-purpose jack**

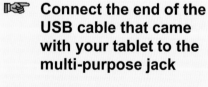 **Connect the other end to one of your computer's USB ports**

On some tablets you will find the multi-purpose jack on the small side of the tablet.

Source: Samsung Galaxy Tab 4 User Guide

You will probably see a window with a message that the device is being installed. A short while later, the device will be ready for use.

In the *Smart Switch* window you can see that there is a connection with the Samsung Galaxy Tab:

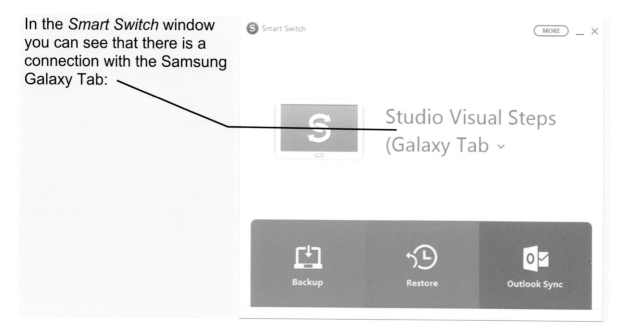

1.11 Safely Disconnecting the Samsung Galaxy Tab

If you want to disconnect the Samsung Galaxy Tab, you need to make sure no data is being transferred between the device and the computer. If that is the case, the data on your computer may be damaged. If you see a message at the bottom of the screen that the transfer has finished, there will no longer be any data traffic. This is how you close the *Smart Switch* program:

In the top right-hand corner of the window:

☞ **Click** ✕

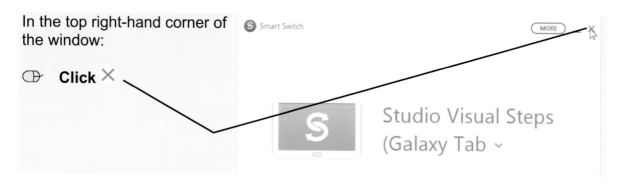

The *Smart Switch* will be closed. Now you can safely disconnect the Samsung Galaxy Tab:

☞ **Disconnect the Samsung Galaxy Tab**

You will be using *Smart Switch* again later on in this book. You can also read about things you can do with *Smart Switch* in the *Tips* at the back of this chapter and of other chapters.

1.12 Creating and Adding a Google Account

Many *Google* and *Android* functions require a *Google* account. A *Google* account is a combination of an email address and a password. In this section you are going to create a new *Google* account. If you already have a *Google* account, you can use it with your Tab.

☞ **Unlock the Samsung Galaxy Tab** 👣⁹

☞ **Tap** ▦ **and** Settings

☞ **If necessary, tap** GENERAL

☞ **Tap + Add account**

Select the *Google* account:

☞ **Tap** 8 **Google**

Now you might see a screen with a Checking info message. Just wait a short while and this screen will disappear.

If you already have a *Google* account:

👉 **Tap** Enter your email

You will see the onscreen keyboard:

⌨ **Type the data**

👉 **Tap** NEXT ›

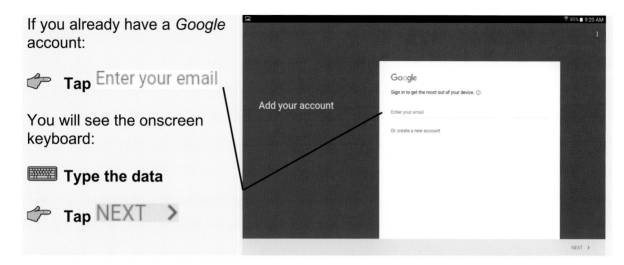

👉 **Follow the instructions and continue with the next section**

To create a new account:

👉 **Tap**

Or create a new account

First, enter your first and last name:

The cursor is already positioned in the First name field:

⌨ **Type your first name**

👉 **Tap** NEXT ›

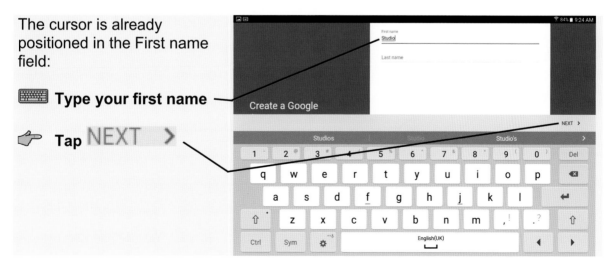

Type your last name

☞ **Tap NEXT** >

You can choose your own user name. This name consists of an email address ending in @gmail.com.

Type the desired user name

☞ **Tap NEXT** >

❊ HELP! User name is already in use.

If the user name you have entered is already being used by someone else, you will see this message This username is not available.

You will see a list of suggestions below the username you entered:

Google will provide some suggestions for available user names:

☞ **Tap a name in the list**

If you decide not to use the suggestion, you can type a different name.

☞ **Tap NEXT** >

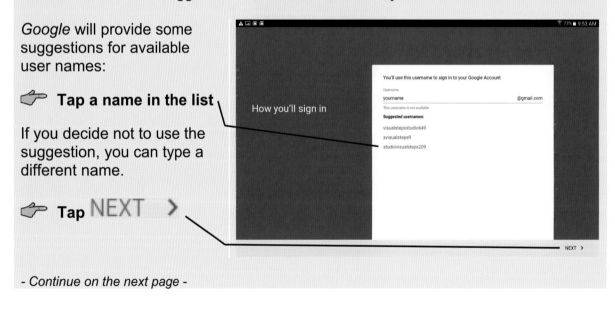

- Continue on the next page -

You will see a screen with the confirmation of your user name:

☞ **Tap** NEXT ❯

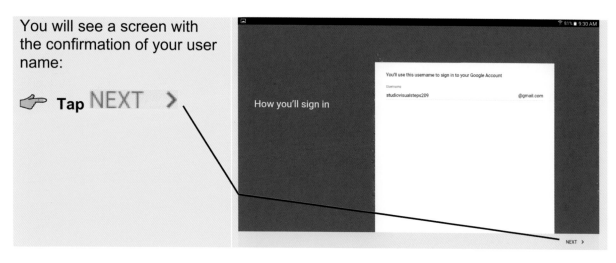

The password that goes with your *Google* account needs to consist of at least eight characters. It is recommended to use a combination of capital and lowercase letters, numbers, and even special characters for your password.

⌨ **Type the desired password**

☞ **Tap** NEXT ❯

You will need to confirm the password:

☞ **Tap** Confirm password

⌨ **Re-type the password**

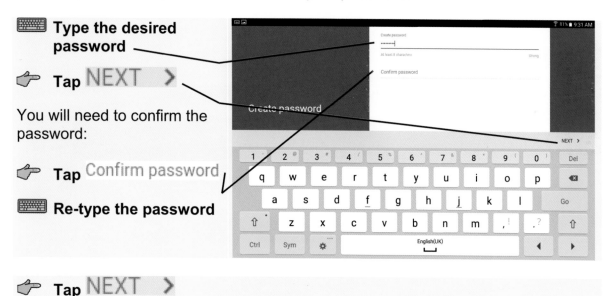

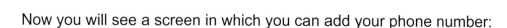

☞ **Tap** NEXT ❯

Now you will see a screen in which you can add your phone number:

For now, this will not be necessary.

☞ **Tap** Skip

Now you will see a screen concerning Privacy and Terms:

To see the entire text:

☞ **Tap** MORE ∨

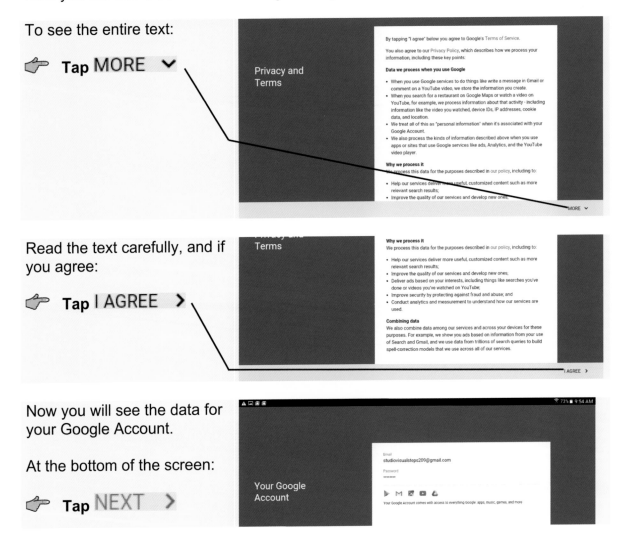

Read the text carefully, and if you agree:

☞ **Tap** I AGREE ❯

Now you will see the data for your Google Account.

At the bottom of the screen:

☞ **Tap** NEXT ❯

You may see a *Checking info* screen. Just wait until this screen disappears.

Now you will see the *Google services* screen:

Leave the box ☑ by
Back up your device's apps, app
checked.

☞ **Tap** NEXT ❯

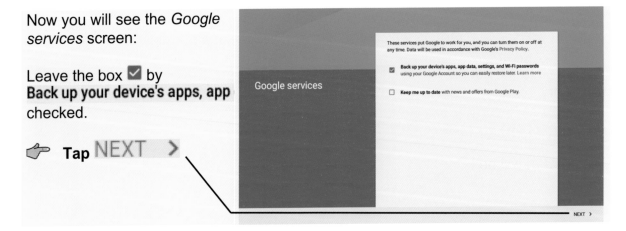

On this screen you can set up a payment method. For now this will not be necessary.

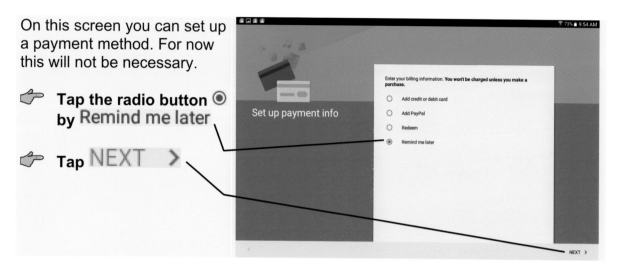

☞ **Tap the radio button** ◉ **by** Remind me later

☞ **Tap** NEXT >

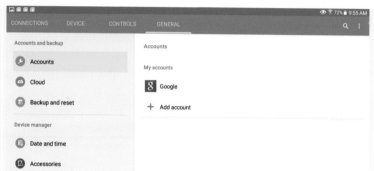

A connection will be established with *Google* and your account will be saved.

Now you will see the *Settings* screen with your new Google account:

Your new *Google* account has been added. You can go back to the home screen:

☞ **Press the Home button**

1.13 Locking or Turning Off the Samsung Galaxy Tab

Once you have finished working on the Samsung Galaxy Tab, you can either lock or completely turn off the tablet. If you lock it, the Samsung Galaxy Tab will still be turned on, but will consume less energy. If you have turned off Wi-Fi or the mobile data network, the Tab will hardly use any power at all. This is how you lock the Samsung Galaxy Tab:

☞ **Press the Power/Lock button** ⓘ

The screen will be turned off and will no longer react to touch gestures.

If you want to turn off the Samsung Galaxy Tab completely, you need to do it like this:

 **Press the Power/Lock button**  **and hold it down for a few seconds**

You will need to confirm this action:

☞ **Tap** ⏻   Power off

☞ **Tap** POWER OFF

The Samsung Galaxy Tab will turn off.

In future, you can choose whether to lock or turn off the Samsung Galaxy Tab. In this chapter you have become acquainted with the main components of the Samsung Galaxy Tab and learned some of the basic operations for using this device. You can find additional information in the *Background Information* and *Tips* sections.

1.14 Background Information

Dictionary

Airplane mode   If your Tab is set to this mode, you will not have access to the Internet and will not be able to use any Bluetooth devices.

Android   A mobile operating system for cell phones, smartphones, tablets and other devices. *Android* is not linked to a single, specific manufacturer. *Google* places *Android* at the disposal of mobile device manufacturers for free. Many manufacturers of smartphones and tablets install their own user interfaces to their devices. This means that tablets from different manufacturers will look and function differently, even though they use the same version of *Android*.

App   Short for *application*, a program for the Samsung Galaxy Tab.

App icons   Colored symbols that can be used to open various apps on the Samsung Galaxy Tab.

Back button   The ⟲ button on the Tab. It lets you go back to the previous screen.

Bluetooth   An open wireless technology standard for exchanging data between devices over short distances. For example, you can use Bluetooth to connect a wireless keyboard or a headset to the Samsung Galaxy Tab.

Dropbox   With this app you can easily store and share photos and documents. You can take a picture with your Tab, save it, and open it on your computer, provided you have installed *Dropbox* on your computer as well.

EDGE   Short for *Enhanced Data Rates for GSM Evolution*. This is an extension of GPRS, which enables higher speed rates for data transmission. The EDGE service is widely available in the USA, but in Europe there is limited availability in some countries.

- Continue on the next page -

Firmware
Software that is embedded in the hardware. The name firmware indicates that the content is quite firm and exists on the boundary between software (easily re-writable and accessible) and hardware (basically unchangeable).

Google account
A combination of a user name and a password, that provides access to *Google* and *Android* functions and services.

GPRS
Short for *General Packet Radio Service*. A technology that offers an extension of the existing gsm network. This technology enables users to send and receive mobile data much faster, more efficiently and cheaper.

Home button
The button on the Tab (also called Home key) with which you can go back to the home screen. You can also use this button to wake up the Tab from sleep mode.

Home screen
The screen filled with widgets and app icons, that you see when you turn on and unlock the Samsung Galaxy Tab.

Location services
With location services, apps such as *Maps* can collect and use data regarding your current location. The collected location data is not linked to your personal data.

Lock
You can lock the Samsung Galaxy Tab by turning off the screen with the Power/Lock button, when you do not need to use the device. If the Samsung Galaxy Tab is locked, nothing will happen when you touch the screen. Music playback will continue as usual. And you will still be able to use the volume control buttons.

Lock screen
The screen that appears when you turn on the Samsung Galaxy Tab. You will need to unlock the Tab on this screen, before you can use the device.

Micro SD card
A Micro SD memory card, sized 15 x 11 x 1 mm (about the size of a fingernail), often used in smartphones and tablets. The Tab is equipped with a Micro SD card slot. By inserting a Micro SD card you can expand the Tab's memory.

- Continue on the next page -

Play Store	An online store where you can download free and paid apps.
Power/Lock button	The button, with which you can lock, unlock, and turn on or turn off the Samsung Galaxy Tab.
Recent apps button	The [▭] button on the Tab that lets you quickly switch between recently used apps.
Roaming, data roaming	Using the mobile data network of a different service provider, in case your own provider's network is not available. This may result in high expenses if you do this abroad.
Samsung account	A combination of a user name and a password with which users can gain access to specific services offered by Samsung.
Samsung Galaxy Tab	The Samsung Galaxy Tab is a portable multimedia device (tablet computer) made by Samsung. There are tablets available with a 7.0 up to 18.4 inch multi-touch screen.
SIM card	SIM stands for *Subscriber Identity Module*. The SIM card is the (small) chip card that is provided by your mobile service provider and that you need to insert in your tablet or cell phone. Usually you will need to do this yourself.
Simlock	A simlock is a lock that has been installed in a cell phone, or any other mobile device, and is intended to prevent the user from inserting a SIM card issued by a different phone service provider. These simlocks are often installed because the phones are offered at very low prices (supported and paid for by the providers) in order to attract and retain customers. The Samsung Galaxy Tab Wi-Fi + 3G/4G is simlock free.
Smart stay	If the *Smart stay* option is enabled, the screen will remain turned on as long as you are watching it.
Smart Switch	A program with which you can manage the content of the Samsung Galaxy Tab and other Samsung devices.
Synchronize	Literally, this means equalizing. When you synchronize your Tab with *Smart Switch*, the content will be placed in a folder on your computer.

- Continue on the next page -

Tablet computer, tablet	A tablet computer is a computer with no separate casing or keyboard. It can be fully operated through the multi-touch screen.
Timeout screen	A function that will turn off and lock the Samsung Galaxy Tab by default after 30 seconds of inactivity.
Widget	Small applications that provide information and useful functions.
Wi-Fi	Wireless network for the Internet.
3G	The third generation of data transmission standards for cell phones and tablets. Because of the higher speed, 3G offers more options than previous standards. With 3G you can make use of services such as making phone calls through the Internet.
4G	4G is the fourth generation of mobile data transmission standards for cell phones and tablets. With 4G you can make use of services such as making phone calls through the Internet, among other things. It is faster than 3G.

Source: User manual Samsung Galaxy Tab, Wikipedia

1.15 Tips

 Tip

Set up sounds

Your Tab makes several noises when certain events occur. For instance, when you receive an email or a notification, or when you are using the keyboard. You can determine which sounds you do and do not want to hear. You can do this with the *Settings* app:

☞ **Open the *Settings* app** ⬯⬯⁵

☞ **If necessary, tap** DEVICE

☞ **If necessary, tap** 🔊 **Sounds and notifications**

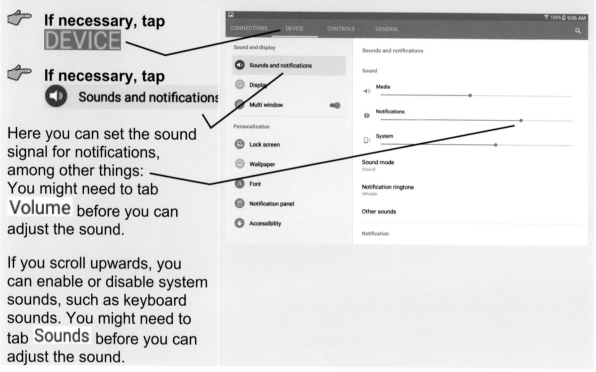

Here you can set the sound signal for notifications, among other things:
You might need to tab Volume before you can adjust the sound.

If you scroll upwards, you can enable or disable system sounds, such as keyboard sounds. You might need to tab Sounds before you can adjust the sound.

 Tip

Timeout screen

By default, your tablet will be locked after 30 seconds of inactivity. This setting will save battery energy, but you might find it easier to keep the Samsung Galaxy Tab unlocked for a little while longer:

☞ **Open the *Settings* app** ⬯⬯⁵

- Continue on the next page -

☞ **If necessary, tap DEVICE**

☞ **Tap** Display

☞ **Tap Screen timeout**

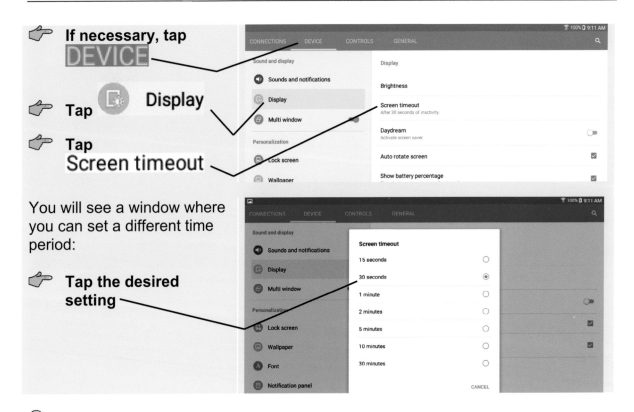

You will see a window where you can set a different time period:

☞ **Tap the desired setting**

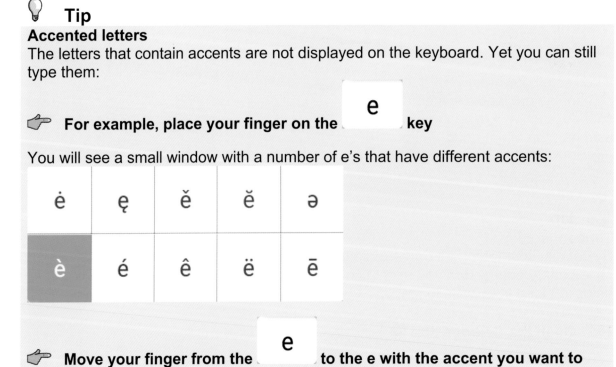

💡 **Tip**

Accented letters

The letters that contain accents are not displayed on the keyboard. Yet you can still type them:

☞ **For example, place your finger on the** e **key**

You will see a small window with a number of e's that have different accents:

ė	ę	ě	ĕ	ə
è	é	ê	ë	ē

☞ **Move your finger from the** e **to the e with the accent you want to use**

- Continue on the next page -

Please note: if you release ![e] first, the small window will disappear.

☞ **Release the key**

The accented e will appear in the text.

💡 **Tip**
Typing with Google voice control
The Tab is equipped with the *Google Voice* function. This function converts speech to text:

☞ **Open a new memo** 🐾10

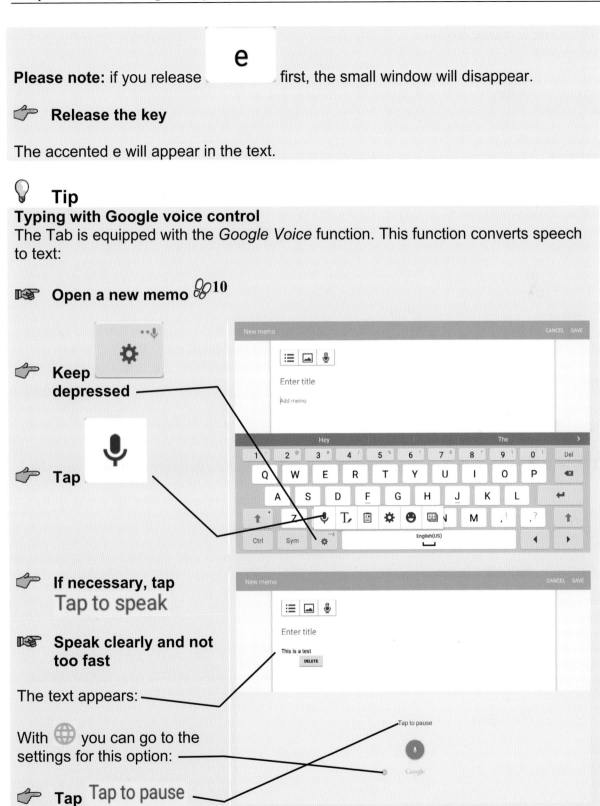

☞ **Keep depressed**

☞ **Tap**

☞ **If necessary, tap** Tap to speak

☞ **Speak clearly and not too fast**

The text appears:

With 🌐 you can go to the settings for this option:

☞ **Tap** Tap to pause

- Continue on the next page -

To go back to the onscreen keyboard:

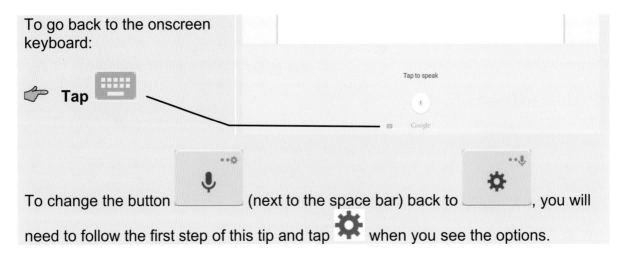

☞ **Tap** ⌨

To change the button 🎤 (next to the space bar) back to ⚙, you will need to follow the first step of this tip and tap ⚙ when you see the options.

💡 **Tip**

Lock the screen with a pattern

When you turn on the tablet, you drag your finger over the screen, in order to unlock the device. Of course, anyone can do this. But you can protect your tablet even better. For example, with a PIN, a password, or a pattern. You can set a pattern like this:

☞ **Open the** *Settings* **app** 👣5

☞ **If necessary, tap** DEVICE

☞ **Tap** 🔒 **Lock screen**

Screen lock

☞ **Tap** Swipe

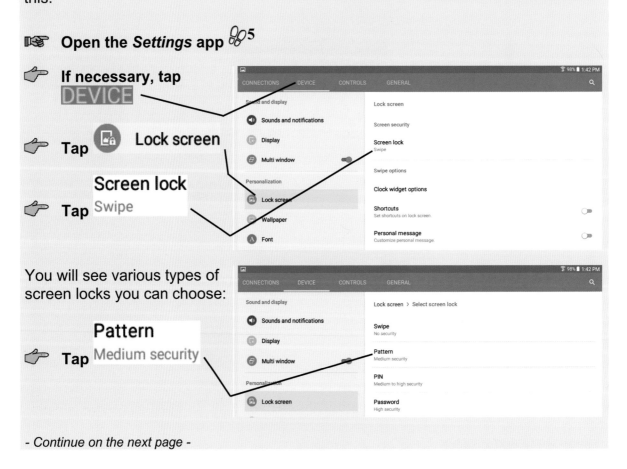

You will see various types of screen locks you can choose:

Pattern

☞ **Tap** Medium security

- Continue on the next page -

☞ **Drag a pattern that connects at least four circles** ⎯⎯⎯⎯

You can pick a different pattern from the one in this example, of course:

☞ **Tap** CONTINUE

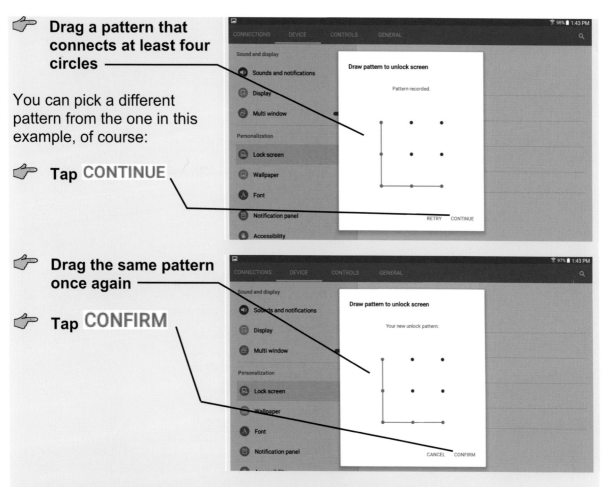

☞ **Drag the same pattern once again** ⎯⎯⎯

☞ **Tap** CONFIRM

By way of an extra security check, you will be asked to choose a PIN consisting of four digits. With this PIN you can unlock your tablet as well, in case you have forgotten the pattern:

⌨ **Type a PIN** ⎯⎯⎯⎯

☞ **Tap** Done

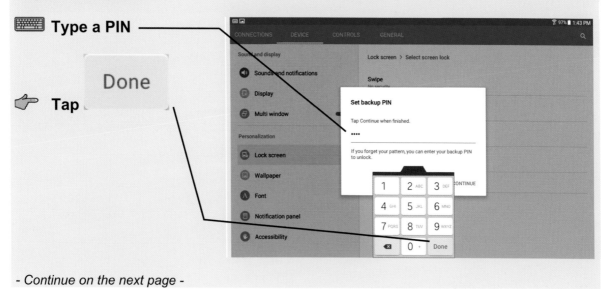

- Continue on the next page -

Now you need to confirm the PIN:

▦ **Re-type the PIN**

☞ **Tap** Done

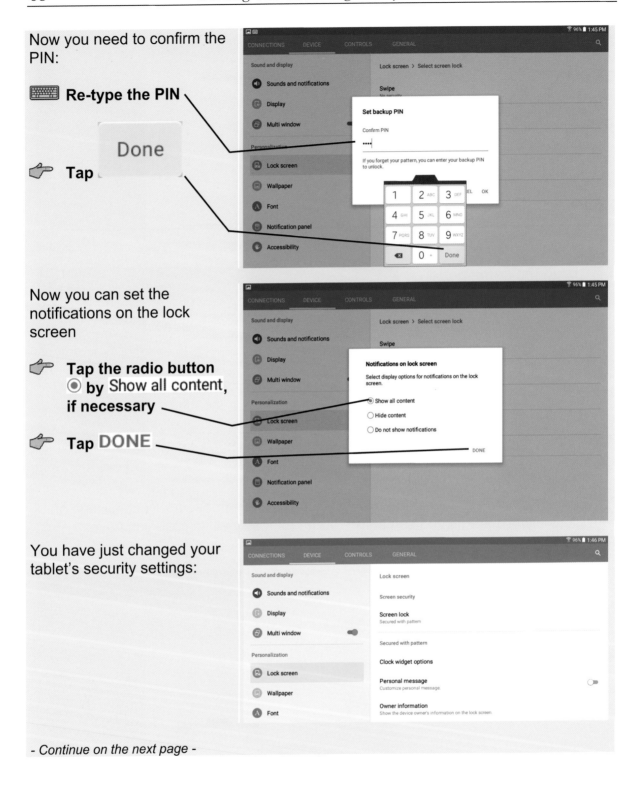

Now you can set the notifications on the lock screen

☞ **Tap the radio button ⊙ by** Show all content, **if necessary**

☞ **Tap** DONE

You have just changed your tablet's security settings:

- Continue on the next page -

Now you are going to check if it works:

☞ **Press the Home button**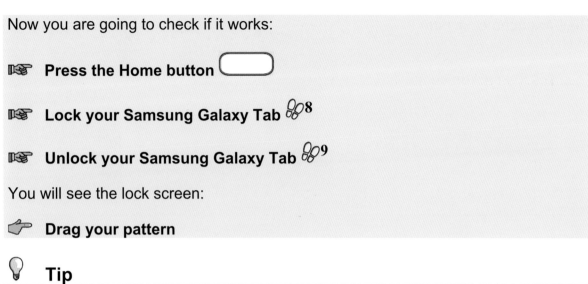

☞ **Lock your Samsung Galaxy Tab** 🐾[8]

☞ **Unlock your Samsung Galaxy Tab** 🐾[9]

You will see the lock screen:

☞ **Drag your pattern**

 Tip

Create a backup with Smart Switch
In the *Smart Switch* program you can manually create a backup copy of your Samsung Galaxy Tab. This is how you do it.
On your computer:

☞ **Open *Smart Switch*** 🐾[11]

☞ **Connect the Samsung Galaxy Tab to the computer, laptop or notebook**

You will see the *Smart Switch* home screen:

☞ **Click**

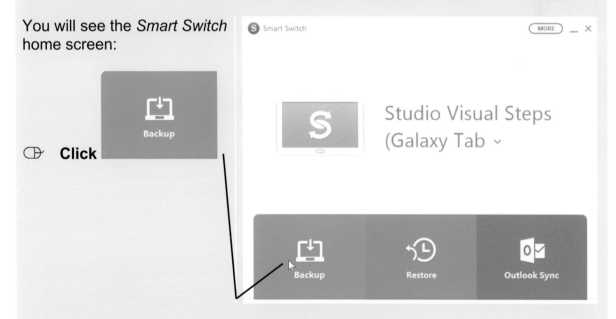

Now a backup copy is created of all the files on the tablet.

- Continue on the next page -

The backup process has finished:

To check the backup items:

☞ **Click**

Check backup items

On the next screen, all the backup items are displayed:

With the

View backup folder

button, the folder containing the backup copy will be opened in *File Explorer*.

To confirm the backup:

☞ **Click** **Confirm**

Now you will need to confirm the backup once more:

☞ **Click** **Confirm**

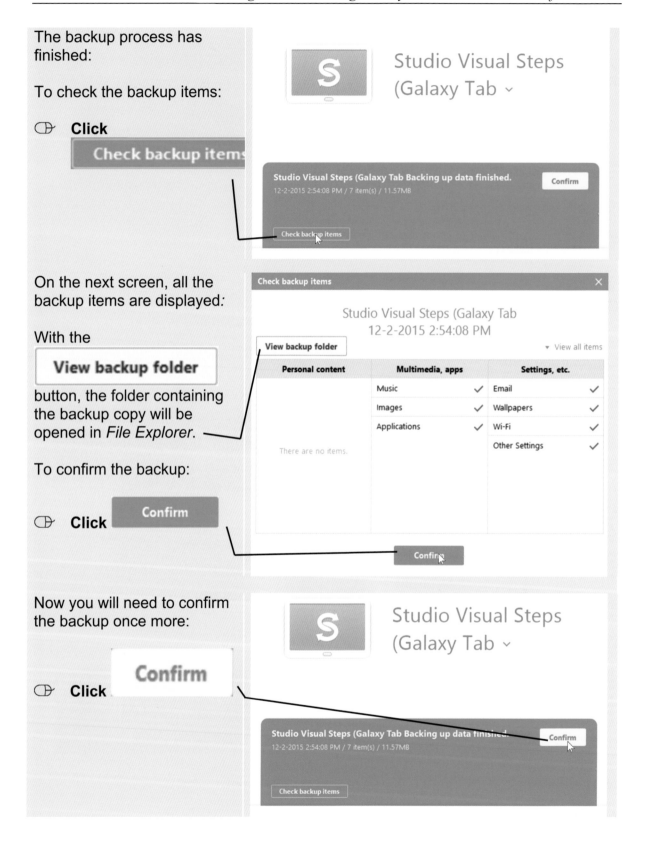

Tip

Restore a backup with Smart Switch

If you experience any problems with your tablet, you can restore a previously created backup. Here is how you do that on your computer:

☞ **Open *Smart Switch* ⑳11**

☞ **Connect the Samsung Galaxy Tab to the computer or notebook**

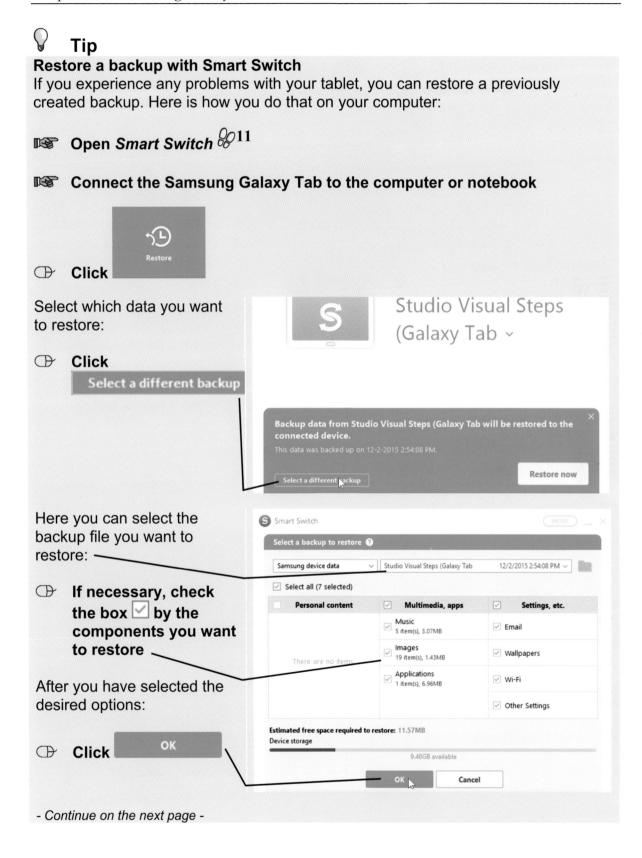

Click

Select which data you want to restore:

Click

Select a different backup

Here you can select the backup file you want to restore:

If necessary, check the box ☑ by the components you want to restore

After you have selected the desired options:

Click OK

- Continue on the next page -

☞ **Click**

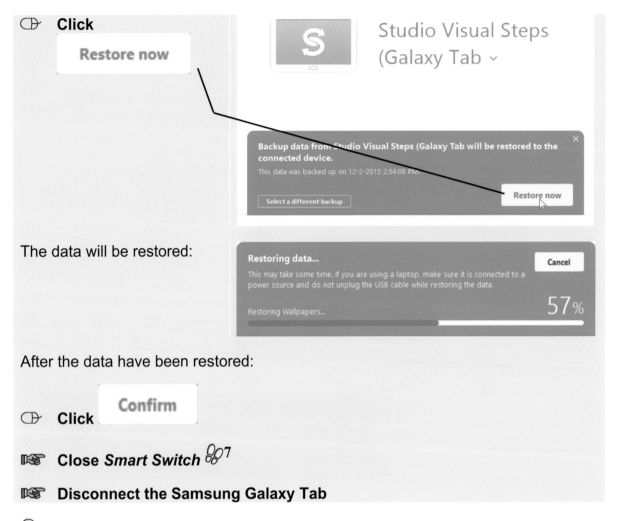

The data will be restored:

After the data have been restored:

☞ **Click**

☞ **Close** *Smart Switch* ◊◊7

☞ **Disconnect the Samsung Galaxy Tab**

💡 **Tip**

Upgrading the Tab firmware through Smart Switch
Previously, you have read how to download and install a software update to your Tab using Wi-Fi. With *Smart Switch* you can upgrade the *firmware* on your device. Firmware is software that is embedded in the hardware. The name 'firmware' indicates that the content is firm and is something between software (easy to overwrite) and hardware (basically not overwritable).

☞ **Open** *Smart Switch* ◊◊11

☞ **Connect the Samsung Galaxy Tab to the computer or notebook**

- Continue on the next page -

If an update is available, you will see a message on the *Smart Switch* home screen.

☞ **Create a backup of the data on your tablet as described in the previous** ***Tip***

☞ **Click** Update.

☞ **Follow the instructions in the windows**

♡ Tip

Smart stay

The Tab has a *Smart stay* function. This means that the Tab can detect whether you are watching the screen or not. If you are not watching the screen, the screen will turn dark after a while, and you will need to unlock the device.

You can easily enable and disable the *Smart stay* function. You can do this in the *Notification Panel*:

☞ **Open the *Notification Panel*** 1

In order to disable *Smart stay*:

👉 **Tap**

👉 **Tap** Smart stay

Now *Smart stay* is disabled.

In order to enable *Smart stay* again:

👉 **Tap** Smart stay

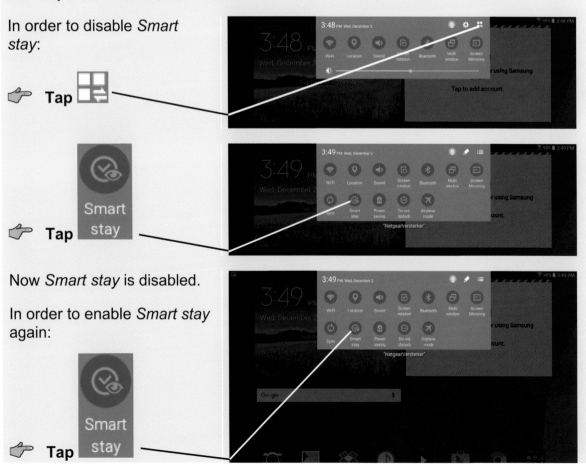

Tip

Add new users

By adding new users, you can let other people use your Tab with their own preferences. You can also create a restricted profile which will allow other users only limited access to apps and content. This is how to add a new user:

☞ **Open the *Settings* app**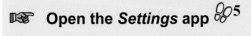

☞ **If necessary, tap** GENERAL

👉 **Tap** 👤 **Users**

👉 **Tap**
  ＋ **Add user or profile**

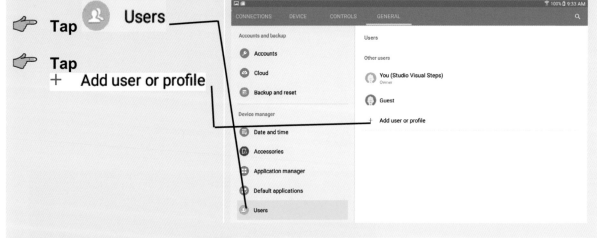

In the *Add* window:

👉 **Tap** User

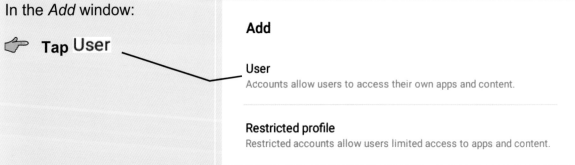

Add

User
Accounts allow users to access their own apps and content.

Restricted profile
Restricted accounts allow users limited access to apps and content.

- Continue on the next page -

You will see information on this process:

 **Tap OK**

Add user

You can share this device with other people by creating additional users. Users have their own space, which they can customize with their own apps, wallpaper and so on. Users can also adjust device settings like Wi-Fi that affect everyone.

After you create a new user, that person needs to go through a setup process.

Any user can accept updated app permissions on behalf of all other users.

CANCEL   OK

You will see some information on the set up process. If you want to proceed:

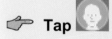 **Tap SET UP NOW**

Set up user

Make sure the user is available to take the device and set up the space.

NOT NOW   SET UP NOW

 Set up the account like you learned in this chapter

You can go to another account like this:

Open the *Notification Panel* &1

Tap

- Continue on the next page -

☞ **Tap the account you want to use**

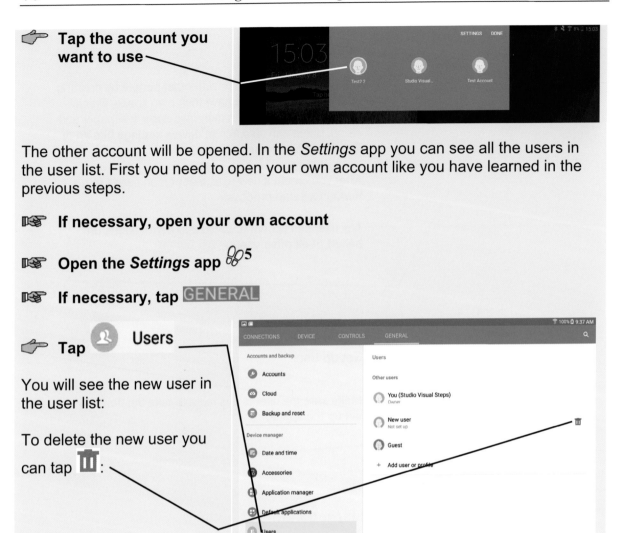

The other account will be opened. In the *Settings* app you can see all the users in the user list. First you need to open your own account like you have learned in the previous steps.

☞ **If necessary, open your own account**

☞ **Open the *Settings* app** 🐾5

☞ **If necessary, tap** GENERAL

☞ **Tap** 👥 **Users**

You will see the new user in the user list:

To delete the new user you can tap 🗑 :

2. Using Email on Your Tablet

Most Samsung Galaxy tablets are equipped with two standard apps for using email: *Gmail* and *Email*. The *Email* app allows you to use the email services from any provider you like. With both apps you can write, send and receive email messages, just like you do on your computer.

In this chapter you will learn how to use the *Email* app. To start using this app, you must first add an email account.

It is easy to use your Samsung Galaxy Tab to compose an email. In this chapter you will practice doing this. You will learn how to select, copy, cut, and paste text on the screen of the Samsung Galaxy Tab. You will also get acquainted with the *Predictive text* function.

Later we will explain how to send, receive and delete email messages.

In this chapter you will learn how to:

- set up an email account in the *Email* app;
- use the *Predictive text* function;
- cut, paste and copy text;
- send an email;
- receive an email;
- move an email to the *Trash*;
- permanently delete an email.

 Please note:

While you are using your Tab, you may see some screens that provide additional information about the operation of an app or the keyboard. You can read the information and tap DONE or OK afterwards.

2.1 Opening Email and Adding an Email Account

In this section you are going to open the *Email* app, and you will learn how to add an Internet service provider's account, for instance, AT&T or T-Mobile. In order to do this, you will need to have the server data, the user name, and the password sent to you by your service provider. If you have an email address ending in outlook.com, hotmail.com, live.com, or gmail.com, you can use any of them to set up an email address for your Tab.

☞ **Turn on ∞⁴ or unlock the Samsung Galaxy Tab ∞⁹**

Open the *Email* app in the screen with the full list of apps. In the bottom right-hand corner of the screen:

☞ **Tap** ⬛

☞ **Tap Email**

You will see a screen where you need to enter some basic information concerning your email account. You can use the onscreen keyboard of your Tab to type this information:

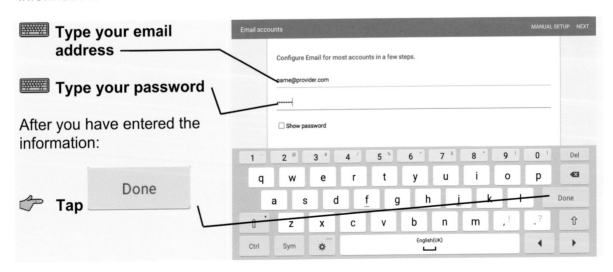

⌨ **Type your email address**

⌨ **Type your password**

After you have entered the information:

☞ **Tap Done**

Now you may need to choose whether you want to set up your account as an *IMAP*, *POP*, or *Microsoft Exchange ActiveSync* account:

- IMAP stands for *Internet Message Access Protocol*. This means that you manage your messages on the mail server. Messages that have been read will still be stored on the mail server, until you delete them. IMAP is useful if you want to manage your email on multiple computers or devices. Your mailbox will look the same on all the devices you use.
  In case you have created folders to arrange your messages, these folders will be present on all the other computers too, and on your Tab. If you want to use IMAP, you need to set up your email account as an IMAP account on all your devices.
- POP stands for *Post Office Protocol*, which is the traditional way of managing email. When you collect your mail, the messages will immediately be deleted from the server. Although the default setting on your Tab for POP accounts is to save a copy of your emails on the server, even after you have retrieved your messages. This means you can always retrieve your messages on your computer as well.
- *Microsoft Exchange ActiveSync*. This technologies enables you to use your Tab to work with the same email, calendars, tasks, and contacts as in the *Microsoft Outlook* email program (part of the *Microsoft Office* suite). This way, you can also access your data when you are travelling. Moreover, *ActiveSync* makes sure that the information on the Tab and in *Microsoft Outlook* is the same. We will not discuss this technology any further in this book.

☞ **If necessary, tap POP3 ACCOUNT or IMAP ACCOUNT**

If you do not see the previous screen:

☞ **Continue on the next page by *Account options* screen**

Now you can enter the information you have received from your Internet service provider:

⌨ **By User name, type the user name**

⌨ **By Password, type your password**

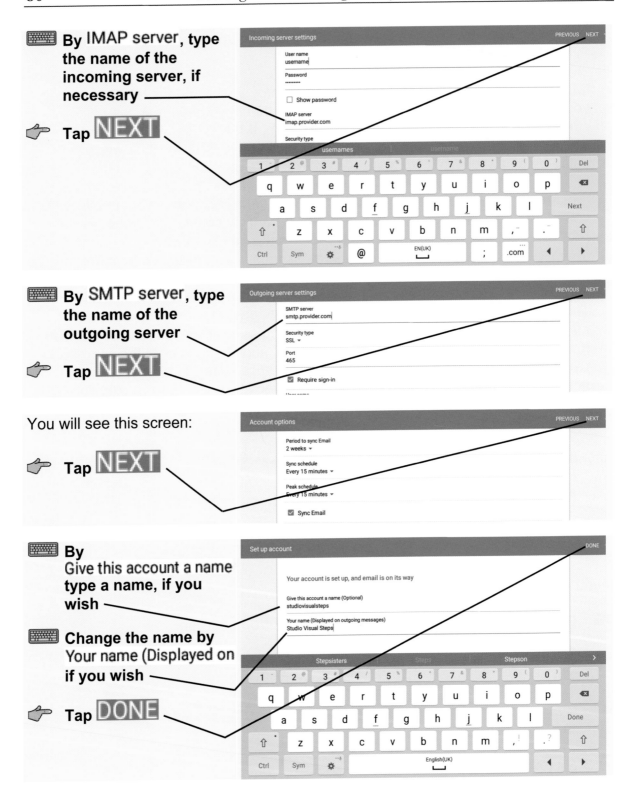

By IMAP server, type the name of the incoming server, if necessary ____

☞ Tap NEXT

By SMTP server, type the name of the outgoing server ____

☞ Tap NEXT

You will see this screen:

☞ Tap NEXT

By Give this account a name type a name, if you wish ____

Change the name by Your name (Displayed on if you wish ____

☞ Tap DONE

You will see the *Email* screen on your tablet:
On some tablets, this screen may look a bit different.

In this example, the inbox already contains emails:

You may not see any messages on your own Tab.

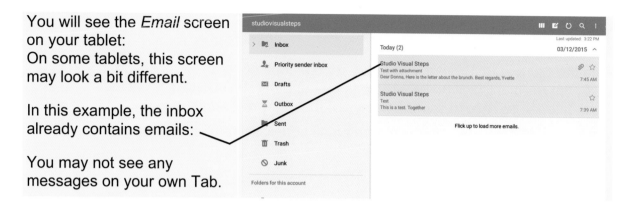

2.2 Sending an Email

To practice using email you can write and send an email message to yourself. Open a new, blank email:

In the top right-hand corner of the screen:

☞ **Tap** 📝

If you don't see this option,

then tap ⬤ at the bottom left of the screen.

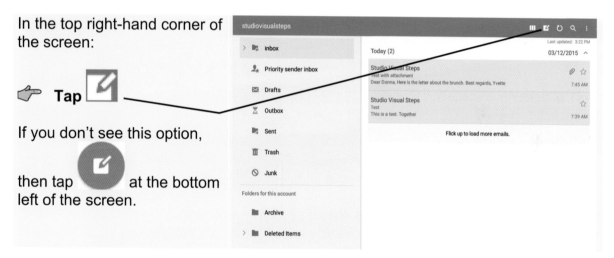

A new message is opened.

⌨ **By** To**, type your email address**

Tip

CC and BCC

With the CC and BCC options you can send a copy of an email message. If you use BCC, the recipients will not be visible to one another. If you use CC, all the recipients will be able to see the names of the other recipients. If you want to use this option, you tap ▼ and enter the email addresses of the recipient(s) on the relevant line.

 Tip

Contacts

If any contacts have been added to the *Contacts* app, you will see a list of names and corresponding email addresses, after you have typed the first two letters of a name. You can quickly add the email address by tapping the name you want to use. In *Chapter 4 Managing Your Contacts, Calendar, and Widgets* you will learn how to fill the contacts' list in the *Contacts* app.

☞ **By** Subject **, type:**
Test

While you are typing, the bar above the keyboard will display all kinds of suggestions for the word you are typing:

This function is called *Predictive text*. While you type, entire words are recommended on the basis of the letters you have already typed. This can save you a lot of typing time. Just try this with the first part of the word 'computer'.

☞ **Tap the white text box**

☞ **Type:** Compu

You will see various suggestions. This is how you accept a suggestion:

☞ **Tap** Computer

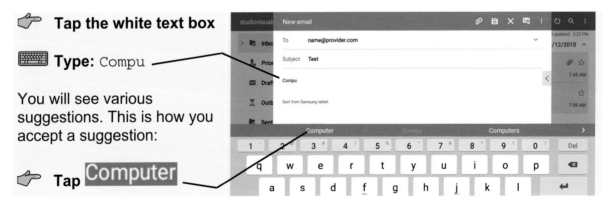

Tip

Accept a correction
A suggested blue correction will also be accepted if you type a period, comma or another punctuation mark.

 Tip

Disable predictive text
In the *Tips* at the end of this chapter you can read how to disable the *Predictive text* function while you are typing.

If you are not satisfied with what you have typed, you can quickly delete the text with the Backspace key:

☞ **Press your finger to** ⟨⊠⟩ **until the text is deleted**

⌨ **Type:** The screen of the Samsung Galaxy Tab is touch-sensitive.

☞ **Tap** ⟨↵⟩ **twice**

In the *Email* app you can also copy, cut and paste text. You can do this with a single word, multiple words or the entire text. This is how you select a word:

☞ **Press your finger to the word** Galaxy

Now the word is selected and you will see blue handles below the word:

☞ **Release the screen**

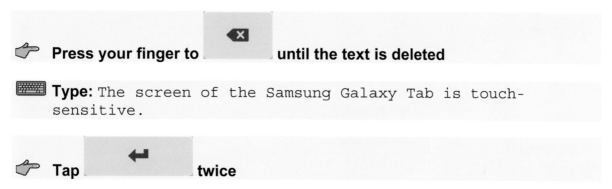

By using the handles you can adjust the selection. For example, you can select the text 'Samsung Galaxy Tab':

Drag the left handle

across Samsung

Drag the right handle

across Tab

The full name has been selected:

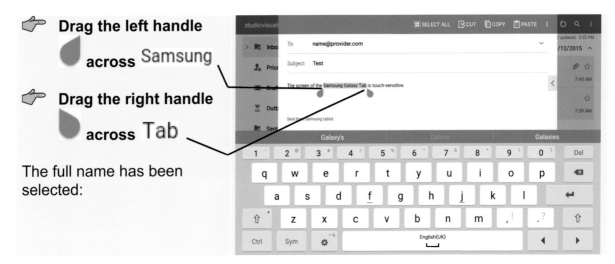

You can cut, copy or replace the selected words. To copy the words:

Tap COPY or
COPY

The words have been copied to the clipboard. This is how you paste them in the text:

Place your finger below the text

You will see a blue bar:

Release the screen

Tap PASTE or
PASTE

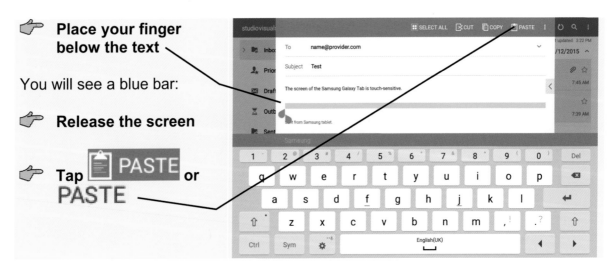

The copied text has been inserted below the first line:

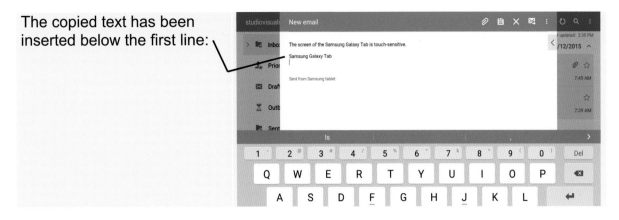

Now you can send your test email:

☞ Tap 〰 or SEND

Your email message is sent, and if the sound on the Samsung Galaxy Tab is turned on, you will hear a sound signal.

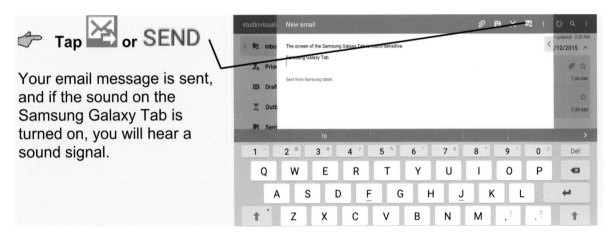

2.3 Receiving an Email

You will receive your message very soon after you have sent it. It will appear at the top of your *Inbox*.

The number indicates that there are unread messages:

☞ If necessary, tap ▨ Inbox (1)

☞ Tap the incoming message

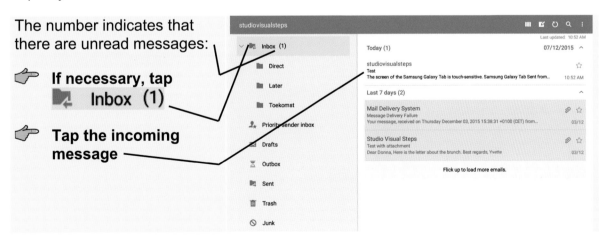

On some tablets the app may
look like this:

 **Tap the incoming
message**

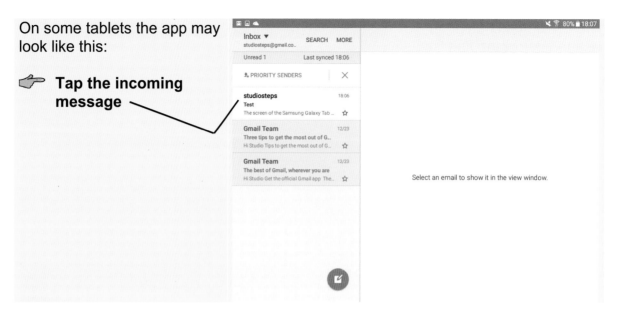

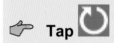 **HELP! I do not receive any email.**

If you do not receive the email right away, you need to tap the icon at the top of your
screen. You can use this icon to retrieve new email:

 Tap 🔄

If you don't see this option:

☞ **Swipe downwards over the side of the screen with the email messages**

You will see the content of
the message:

On the right-hand side of the bar on top, you will see additional icons. This is what
they indicate:

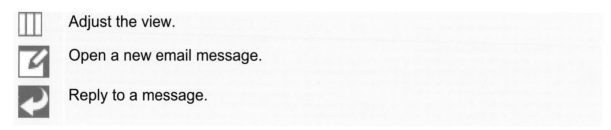

▥   Adjust the view.

▧   Open a new email message.

↩   Reply to a message.

Reply to everyone who has received the message. Appears when an email has been send to more than one person.

 Forward a message.

 Move a message to the *Trash*.

 Open a menu.

When you see the content of the inbox, you will see these icons:

 Search messages.

 Retrieve email.

On some tablets the icons might look slightly different:

The icons are visible at the bottom of the e-mail message: ————

You can show more options by tapping MORE in the top right-hand corner of the screen.

This is how you display the folder list:

☞ **Tap** ⬅ **or by** Inbox

tap ▼

2.4 Deleting an Email

You can delete your test message:

☞ **Tap the message**

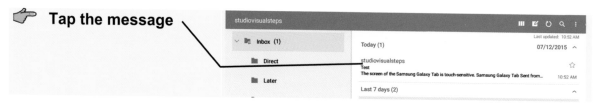

You will see the message again:

☞ Tap 🗑

If you see a different screen you will find 🗑 at the bottom of the screen.

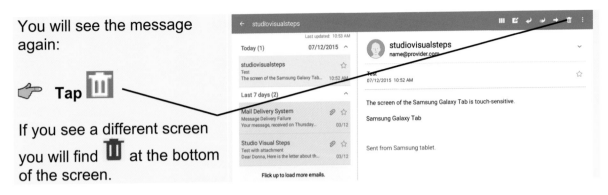

The email has been moved to the *Trash*. You can check to make sure:

☞ If necessary, tap ▼

☞ Tap 🗑 Trash

You will see your deleted message in the *Trash* folder:

☞ Tap the message you want to delete

If you wish, you can also permanently remove the email from the *Trash*:

☞ If you wish, tap 🗑

Or tap 🗑 at the bottom of the screen.

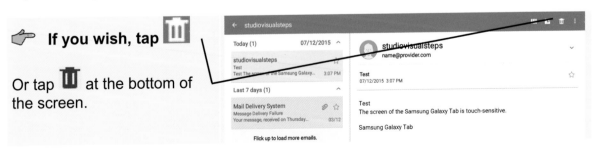

The email has been permanently removed from the *Trash*.

☞ **Go back to the home screen** 𝄐³

☞ **Lock or turn off the Samsung Galaxy Tab, if you wish** 𝄐⁸

In this chapter you have become acquainted with the *Email* app on the Samsung Galaxy Tab. You have learned how to send, receive and delete an email message.

2.5 Background Information

Dictionary

Account	A combination of a user name and a password, that provides access to a specific protected service. A subscription with an Internet service provider is also called an account.
Contacts	A standard app on the Samsung Galaxy Tab, with which you can view and edit your contact data.
Email	A standard app on the Samsung Galaxy Tab, with which you can send and receive email.
Fetch	The traditional way of retrieving new email messages. You open your mail program and connect to the mail server. You can set the program to automatically check for new messages at regular intervals, when the program is opened.
Gmail	A free email service offered by the manufacturers of the well-known *Google* search engine. An app with which you can send and receive the *Gmail* email messages is also called *Gmail*.
Inbox	A folder in which you can view the messages you have received.
Outlook.com	A free email service offered by *Microsoft*.
Predictive text	A function that displays suggestions for the word you are currently typing.
Push	If *push* is set for your email, and is supported by your Internet service provider, the mail server will immediately send new email messages to your email program, right after they have been received. Even if your email program has not been opened and your Tab is locked.
Signature	A standard salutation that is inserted below all your outgoing email.
Trash	A folder that contains the deleted messages. Once you deleted a message from the *Trash*, the message is permanently deleted.

Source: User manual Samsung Galaxy Tab and Gmail

2.6 Tips

 Tip

Add a signature to the messages you send

You can insert a standard text below every email you send. For example, a standard salutation, or your name and address. This text is called your *signature*. This is how you add a signature in the *Email* app:

☞ **Tap** ▯

☞ **If necessary, drag upwards across the menu**

☞ **Tap Settings**

Or if you see a different screen:

☞ **Tap MORE**

☞ **Tap Settings**

☞ **Tap your email account**

☞ **Tap Signature**

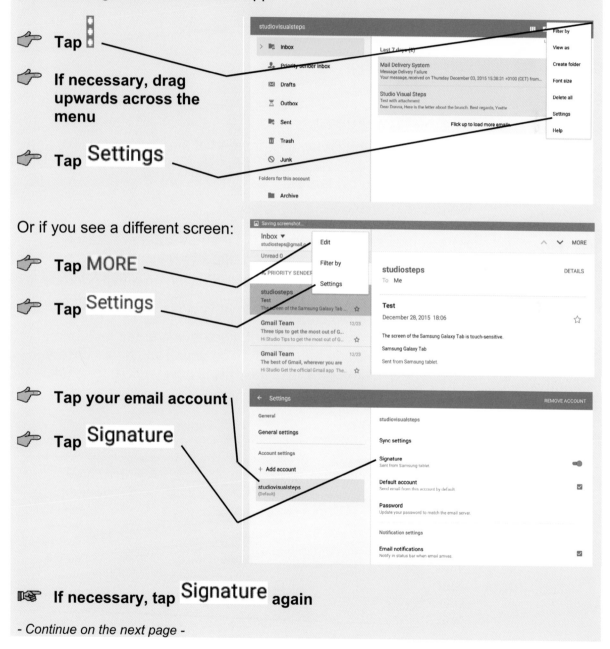

☞ **If necessary, tap Signature again**

- Continue on the next page -

Delete the text ⟋⟍29

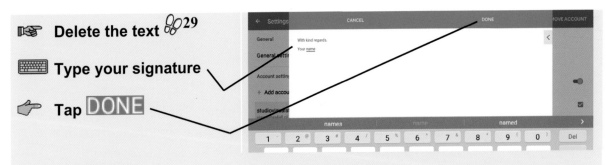

⌨ **Type your signature**

☞ **Tap** DONE

To go back to the *Inbox*:

☞ **Tap** ⬅ **until you see the** *Inbox*

💡 **Tip**

Gmail
If you use *Gmail* you can also use the *Gmail* app, instead of the *Email* app. This app has been especially developed for use with *Google Mail* accounts. You can also use email addresses from some other providers such as outlook.com. This app works in a very similar way as the *Email* app.

💡 **Tip**

Move an email to another folder
You can move email messages to other folders. If you are using an email address ending in @gmail.com, you can create new folders on your Tab. Some email providers, however, will not allow you to create new folders on your Tab. But if you have your email account set up as an IMAP account, and have created folders on your computer, for example, you will see these folders on your Tab. In that case you may also be able to create new folders on your Tab. This is how you create a folder in the *Email* app:

 Open an email message ⟋⟍13

☞ **Tap** ⋮

☞ **If necessary, drag upwards across the menu**

☞ **Tap** Create folder

- Continue on the next page -

☞ **Tap** Root

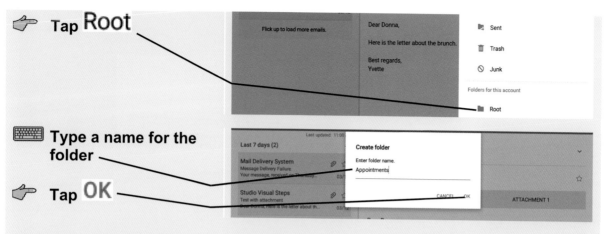

⌨ **Type a name for the folder**

☞ **Tap** OK

The folder will be added.

If you see a different screen you can add a folder like this:

☞ **By** Inbox**, tap** ▼

☞ **Tap** MORE

☞ **Tap** Add folder

☞ **Tap** 📁 Root

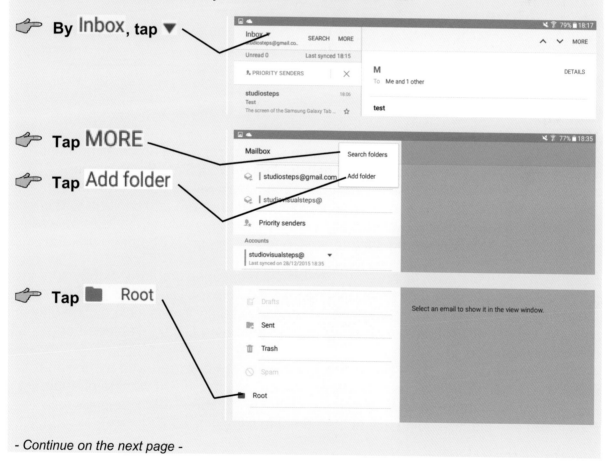

- Continue on the next page -

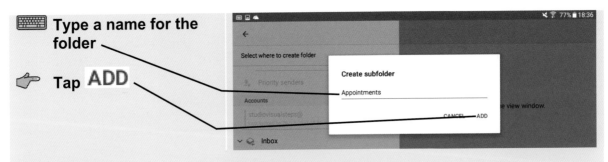

Type a name for the folder

☞ **Tap ADD**

This is how you move an email message to another folder:

☞ **If necessary, open an email message** 👣**13**

☞ **Tap ⋮ or MORE**

☞ **Tap Move**

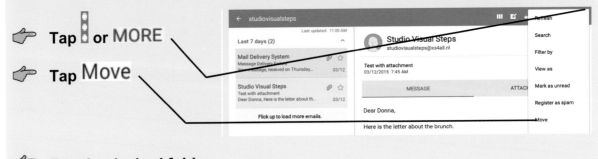

☞ **Tap the desired folder**

💡 **Tip**

Push or fetch
If you also use an email program on your computer, you will be used to retrieving your email with the *fetch* option. You open your email program and connect to the mail server, in order to get new messages. You can set the program to automatically check for new messages at regular intervals, once the program has been opened.

Email works with the *push* technology. New email messages are immediately sent to the *Email* app, right after they have been received by the mail server. Even if the *Email* app has not been opened and your Samsung Galaxy Tab is locked. The only time you will not receive any email, is when your Samsung Galaxy Tab has been completely turned off.

While you were setting up the *Email* app, you have seen a screen with a message about your email being synchronized every fifteen minutes. If you want to change this, you can do it in the window where you view the synchronization settings for *Email*. You can practice doing this at the end of this *Tip*.

- Continue on the next page -

Please note: if you connect to the Internet through a mobile network and you do not have a subscription that offers unlimited data traffic at a fixed rate, it is better to disable the automatic synchronization function of the *Email* app. If this is the case, you will need to pay for the amount of data you use. If you receive email messages with large attachments on your Samsung Galaxy Tab, you may incur additional data fees. You can manually synchronize your email account the next time you are connected with a Wi-Fi network.

This is how you view the synchronization settings for *Email*:

☞ **Open the *Email* app** 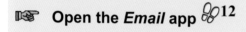12

👉 **Tap** ▐ **or** MORE

👉 **Tap** Settings

👉 **If necessary, tap the account**

👉 **If necessary, tap** Sync settings

If you don't want to the emails to be automatically synchronized:

👉 **If necessary, uncheck the box** ☑ **by** Sync Email

Now your email will no longer be automatically synchronized. You can enable or disable this setting manually with the *Email* app:

👉 **Tap**

💡 **Tip**

Disable predictive text

The *Predictive text* function may sometimes lead to unwanted corrections. The dictionary will not recognize all the words you type, and will still try to come up with suggestions. If you make an occasional typing error, this can lead to rather strange corrections, which you may have accepted without knowing it, by typing a period, comma or a blank space. You can disable the *Predictive text* function if you prefer:

☞ **Open the *Settings* app** 5

- Continue on the next page -

☞ **If necessary, tap**
CONTROLS

☞ **Tap**

Ⓐ **Language and input**

Samsung keyboard
☞ **Tap** Samsung keyboard

🖝 **If necessary, tap** Smart typing

By the predictive text item
you might see a green
(on) or grey/blue (off)
icon. Or you will see the text
On or Off .

You can tap ⬤ to turn the
function off or tap ⭕ to turn it
on.

☞ **If you wish, tap** ⬤

If you don't see then
tap the option first and then
turn it off or on.

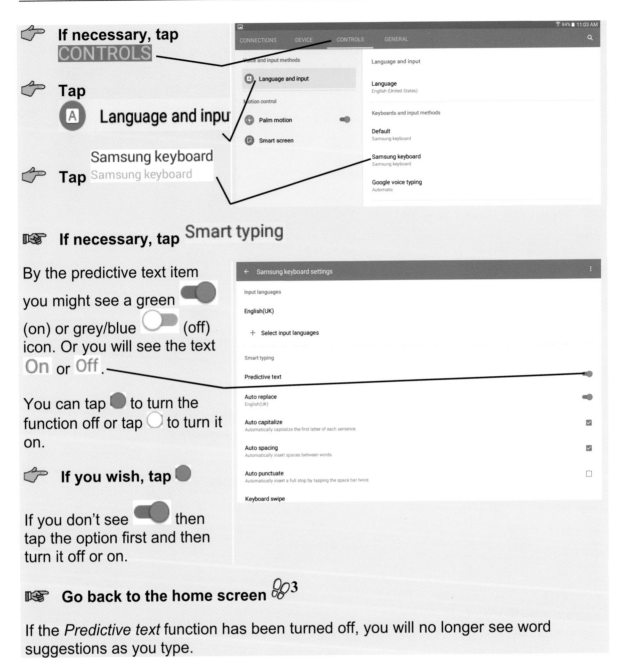

🖝 **Go back to the home screen** 👣3

If the *Predictive text* function has been turned off, you will no longer see word
suggestions as you type.

💡 **Tip**

Create a Samsung account
With a Samsung account you will get access to various online services offered by
Samsung. If you would like to create a Samsung account:

🖝 **Open the *Settings* app** 👣5

- Continue on the next page -

☞ **If necessary, tap** GENERAL

☞ **If necessary, tap** 🔑 **Accounts**

☞ **If necessary, tap** ➕ **Add account**

☞ **Tap** Ⓢ **Samsung account**

Please note: you may need to install some updates first. In order to do this, you need to follow the instructions on the screens.

If you do not yet have an account:

☞ **Tap**
CREATE ACCOUNT

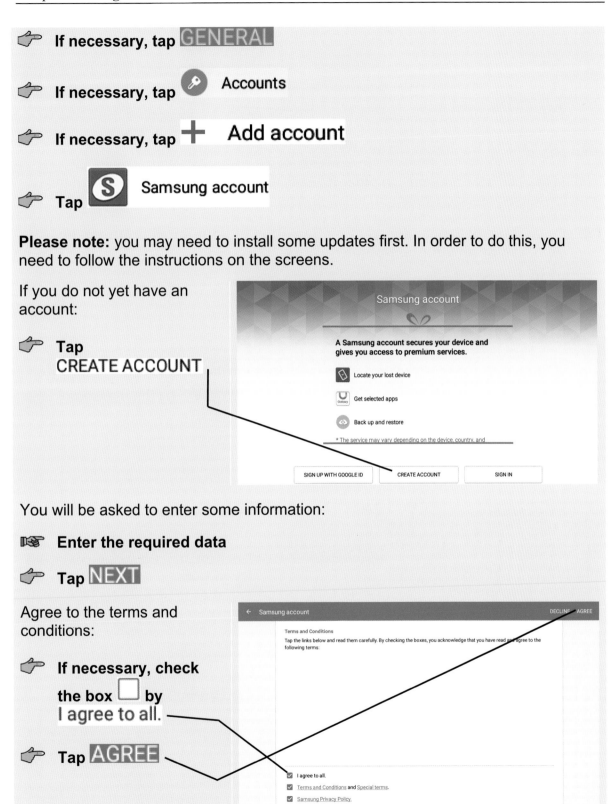

You will be asked to enter some information:

☞ **Enter the required data**

☞ **Tap** NEXT

Agree to the terms and conditions:

☞ **If necessary, check**
the box ☐ **by**
I agree to all.

☞ **Tap** AGREE

- Continue on the next page -

You will be signed in at once, and you will see a Welcome screen:

👉 **Tap CONFIRM**

👉 **Go back to the home screen** 👣³

You have been sent an email, in order to verify your email address. You need to read this email message within 30 days, and open the link in this message.

👉 **Open the email message sent by Samsung in your email program, on your Tab or on your computer**

👉 **Follow the instructions in the email**

💡 **Tip**

Open an attachment
Sometimes, you will also receive an email with an attachment, such as a photo. If the email contains an attachment, you will see a paperclip 📎 by the message in the list.
This is how you open an attachment:

👉 **Open the email message** 👣¹³

👉 **If necessary, tap ATTACHMENTS or tap the attachment**

You will see the attachment(s). In this example, there are two photos:

If you want to view the attachment at once:

👉 **Tap VIEW or PREVIEW**

- Continue on the next page -

☞ **Tap the app in which you want to view the file**

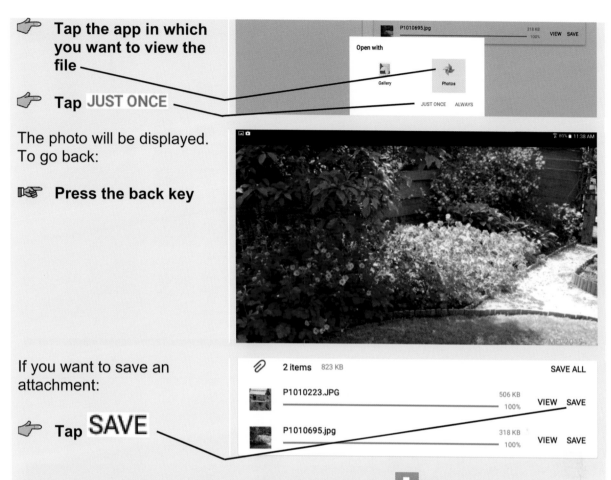

☞ **Tap** JUST ONCE

The photo will be displayed. To go back:

☞ **Press the back key**

If you want to save an attachment:

☞ **Tap SAVE**

The download operation will begin. You can tell by the icon at the top of the screen. You can open the saved attachment by using the *My Files* app. You can find the downloaded file in the *Images* and *Download history* folders. You can also always find photos in the *Gallery* app.

💡 **Tip**

Send an attachment

If you have some photos on your own tablet, you can send these as an attachment to an email. This is how you do it:

☞ **Tap** 📝

☞ **Tap** 📎 **or ATTACH**

- Continue on the next page -

You can add various types of files. In this example we have added an image:

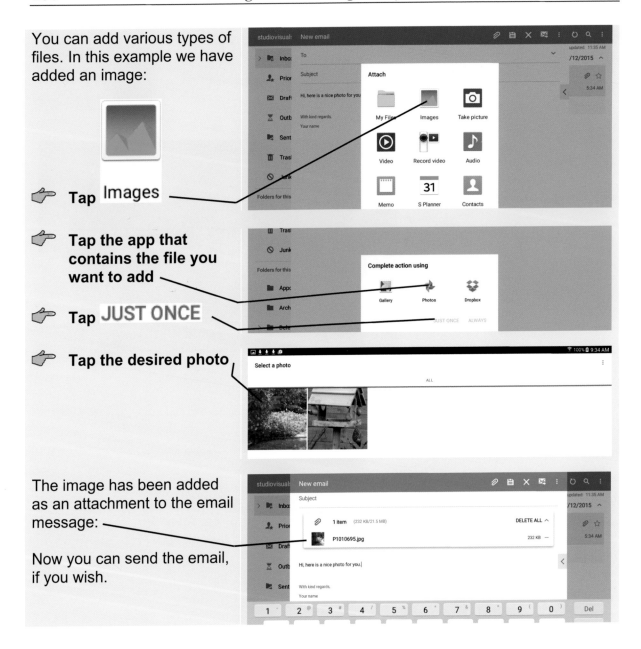

☞ **Tap** Images

☞ **Tap the app that contains the file you want to add**

☞ **Tap** JUST ONCE

☞ **Tap the desired photo**

The image has been added as an attachment to the email message:

Now you can send the email, if you wish.

3. Surfing with Your Tablet

In this chapter you will learn more about the *Internet* app. This is the web browser application that comes with your Samsung Galaxy Tab. You can use this app to surf the Internet on your tablet.

You will learn how to open a web page and you will get acquainted with other touch gestures that allow you to zoom in, zoom out and scroll. We will also explain how to open links (also called hyperlinks) and work with saved web pages.

You can use the *Internet* app to open multiple web pages at once. As you work through this chapter you will see how easy it is to switch between these open pages.

While you are surfing you may see a need to adjust a particular setting. Your Samsung Galaxy Tab is able to execute multiple tasks at once, so you can do this at any time. You can switch from one app to another, recently used app. All of these things are explained in this chapter.

In this chapter you will learn how to:

- open the *Internet* app;
- open a web page;
- zoom in and zoom out;
- scroll;
- open a link on a web page;
- open a link in a new tab;
- switch between open web pages;
- add a bookmark;
- search;
- switch between recently used apps.

 Please note:

While you are using your Tab, you may see some screens that provide additional information about the operation of an app or the keyboard. You can read the information and tap **DONE** or **OK** afterwards.

3.1 Opening the Internet App

This is how you open *Internet*, the app that lets you surf the Internet:

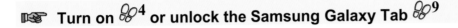 **Turn on** $\mathcal{B}\mathcal{B}^4$ **or unlock the Samsung Galaxy Tab** $\mathcal{B}\mathcal{B}^9$

You can open the *Internet* app:

☞ **If necessary, tap** ▦

☞ **Tap** Internet

The icon for this app may already be shown on the home screen of your own Tab.

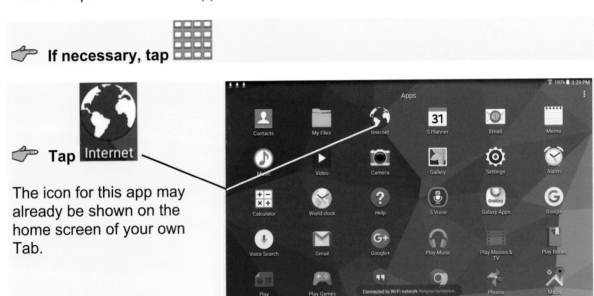

You will see the app's start screen:

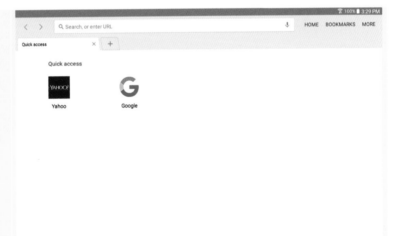

3.2 Opening a Web Page

In order to type a web address, you need to display the onscreen keyboard:

☞ **Tap the address bar**

The onscreen keyboard will appear at the bottom of the screen.

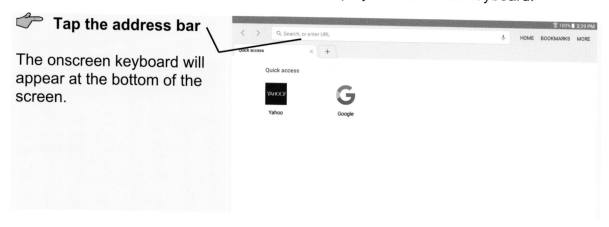

To practice typing an address, you will use the Visual Steps website:

Type: www.

Right away, you will see all kinds of suggestions:

The more letters you type for this address, the more specific the suggestions will become.

Type:

visualsteps.com

When you have finished typing:

☞ **Tap**

Go

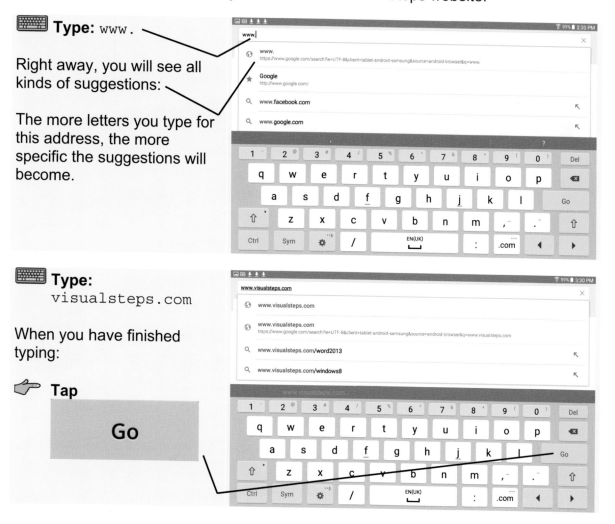

Tip

Use a suggestion

Of course, you can also tap  in the suggestions list.

You will see the Visual Steps website:

3.3 Zooming In and Out

If you think the letters and images on a website are too small, you can zoom in. This is done by double-tapping. You tap the desired location twice, in rapid succession:

☞ **Double-tap the menu on the left-hand side**

🩹 **HELP! A different web page is opened.**

If you do not succeed at double-tapping right away, another window may be opened.

In that case, you can tap 〈 in the top left-hand side of the screen and try again. You can also practice double-tapping on a blank section of the screen.

Now you will see that the size of the web page has increased:

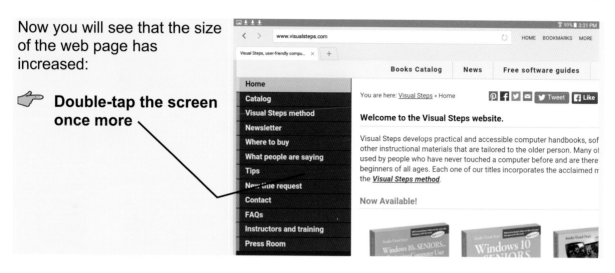

☞ **Double-tap the screen once more**

The screen will zoom out again and display the regular view. There is yet another way of zooming in. You will need to use two fingers to do this:

☞ **Spread your thumb and index finger across the screen**

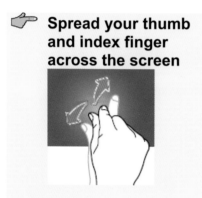

You will see that you can zoom in even further.

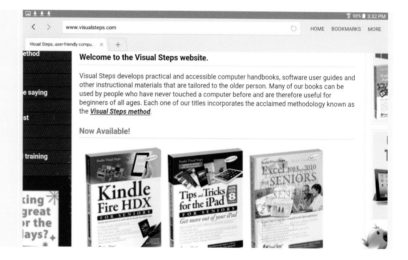

You can zoom out again by doing the opposite (pinching your fingers together):

☞ **Move your thumb and index finger towards each other across the**

screen

Go back to the regular view:

☞ **Double-tap the page**

You will see the regular view again:

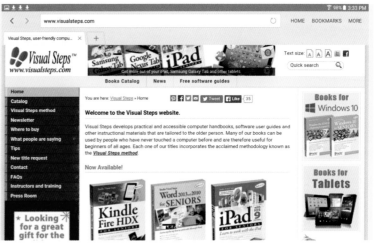

3.4 Scrolling

When you scroll a web page it means you are moving the text and images that appear on the web page across your screen. In this way you can view the full content of a web page. On your tablet you use your fingers to scroll a page:

 Drag your finger a little bit upwards, across the screen

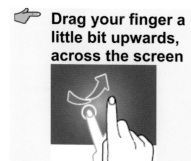

You will see that you are scrolling the page downwards:

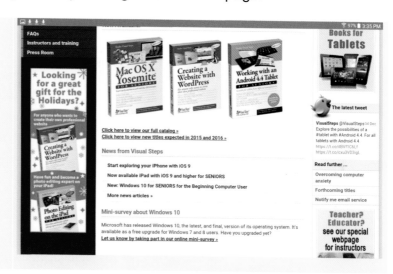

 Drag your finger downwards a bit, across the screen

Now you will be scrolling the page upwards:

💡 **Tip**
Scrolling sideways
On a wide web page you can also scroll sideways by moving your finger across the screen from right to left or from left to right.

If you want to quickly scroll through a long page, you can use a swiping (flicking) gesture:

 Quickly swipe your finger upwards across the screen

You will rapidly scroll down the page:

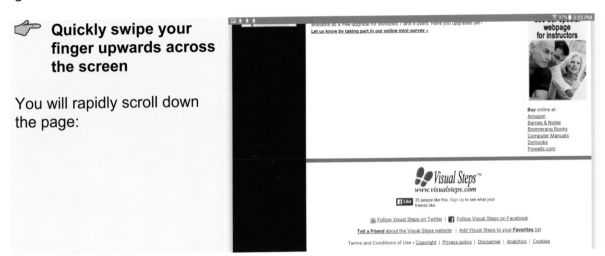

💡 **Tip**

Move in different directions
You can also quickly scroll upwards, to the left, or to the right, if you make the swiping gesture in a different direction.

This is how you quickly go to the top of the page:

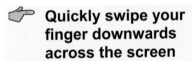 **Quickly swipe your finger downwards across the screen**

You will see the top of the web page again:

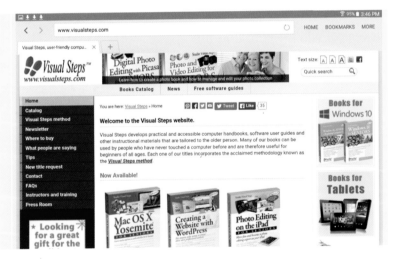

3.5 Opening a Link on a Web Page

If a page contains a link (also called hyperlink), you can open it by tapping the link. Just try it:

A part of the screen may be enlarged:

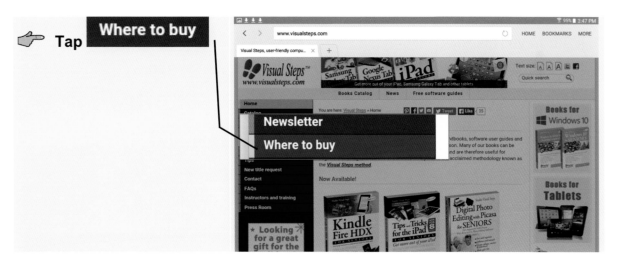

HELP! Tapping the link does not work.

If you find it hard to tap the right link, you can zoom in first. The links will be displayed much larger, and tapping a link will become easier.

Here you can see the web
page about where to find the
Visual Steps books:

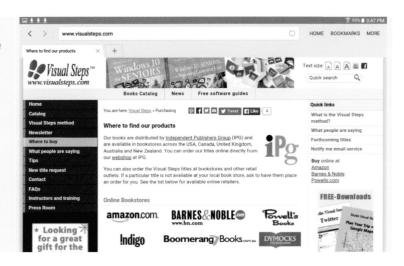

3.6 Opening a Link in a New Tab

You can also open a link in a new tab:

☞ **Place your finger on**
Catalog

After a while you will see a new menu:

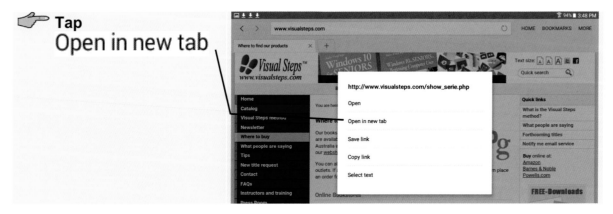

☞ **Tap**
Open in new tab

The linked page will be opened in a new tab:

You will see the page with the Visual Steps catalog:

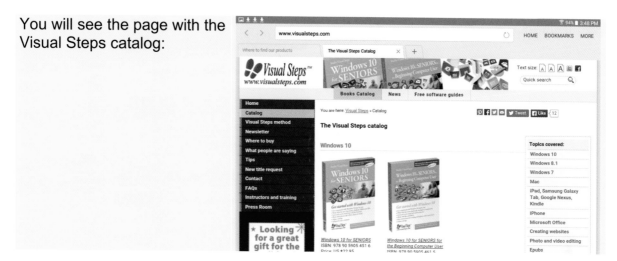

This is how you go back to the first tab:

☞ **Tap**

Where to find our products

Once more, you will see the Where to find our products web page.

☞ **Go to the second tab** 𝒬𝒪**14**

This is how you close an open tab:

☞ **Tap** ✕

Once again, you will see the Visual Steps *Where to find our products* web page:

💡 **Tip**

Open a new, blank tab

You can use the *Internet* app to open a new tab:

☞ **Tap** [+]

You will see the new tab with the default home page.

3.7 Go to a Previous or Next Page

You can go back to the web page you previously visited. You do that like this:

☞ **Tap** ‹

You will see the Visual Steps home page again. You can also go to the next page.

You can use the › button to do this, but for now this will not be necessary.

3.8 Adding a Bookmark

If you want to visit a particular web page in the future, you can add a bookmark for it. A bookmark is the address of a website that has been saved so you can access the web site easier and faster later on. If you set a bookmark, you will not need to type the full web address every time you want to visit the page. Here is how to add a bookmark for a web page that is already open:

☞ Tap **BOOKMARKS**

In the Bookmarks overview, you might see separate folders for your device and a Samsung account. These folders contain a list of bookmarks:

☞ **If necessary, tap**

📁 **My device**

You will see a list of bookmarks:

To add the bookmark of the page that is opened:

☞ Tap **ADD**

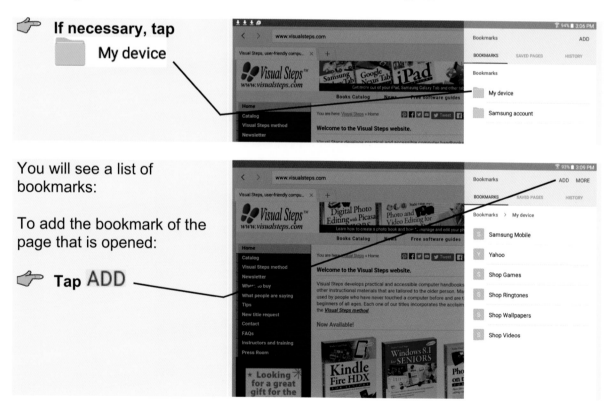

On the right-hand side of the window you can type an easily identifiable name for the web page, if you wish. For now this will not be necessary.
Save the bookmark:

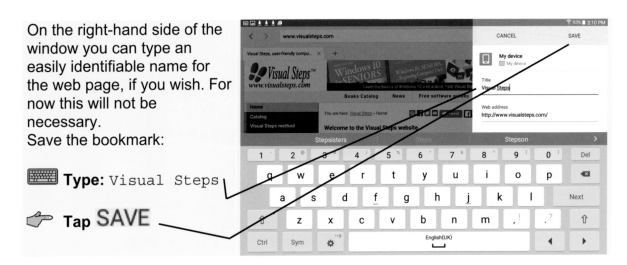

Type: Visual Steps

☞ **Tap SAVE**

The web page has been added to your bookmarks:

☞ **If necessary, drag the screen upwards**

You will see a new bookmark in the list:

Samsung has already added a number of useful bookmarks for you:

☞ **Tap**  **Google**

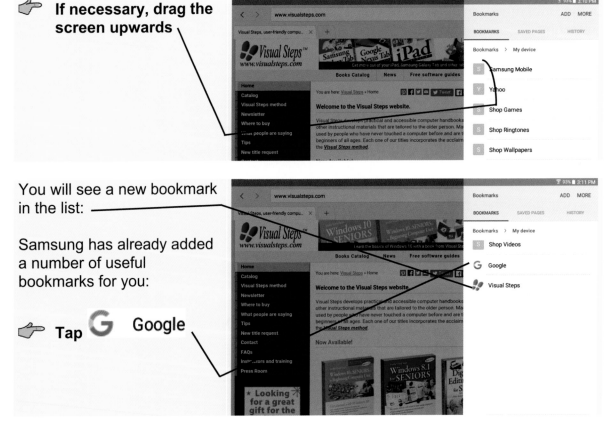

✂ **HELP! I do not see this bookmark.**
If you do not see the bookmark for *Google*, just tap a different bookmark.

You will see the *Google* website:

Go back to the Visual Steps web page:

👉 **Tap** BOOKMARKS

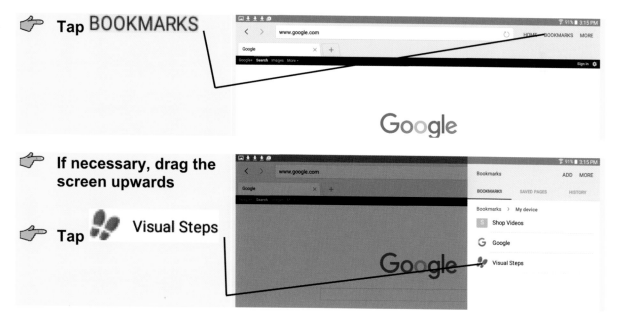

👉 **If necessary, drag the screen upwards**

👉 **Tap** 👣 **Visual Steps**

You will see the Visual Steps web page again.

3.9 Searching

The *Internet* app uses the *Google* search engine. You may already be familiar with using a search box to enter your search terms or phrases, like you do in other Internet browsers, for example on your computer. On the Tab it works in a similar fashion:

👉 **Tap the address bar**

The address bar is replaced by the search box, and the onscreen keyboard appears. Now you can enter your keywords:

Type: Samsung Galaxy Tab sleeve

As you type, you will see all sorts of suggestions for your keywords:

If you want to use one of these suggestions, you just tap it. For now this will not be necessary.

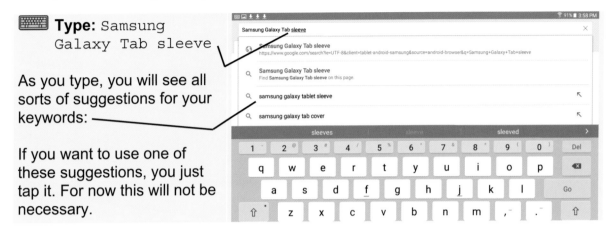

In this example you will use the keywords that you typed:

☞ **Tap** Go

Here you see the search results:

To view one of these results, you need to tap the link. For now this will not be necessary.

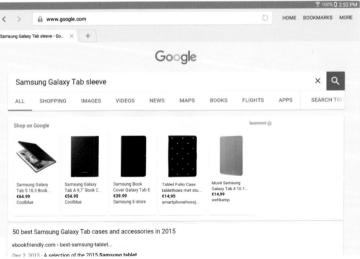

3.10 Switching between Recently Used Apps

You can quickly switch between the apps you have recently used. Just try it:

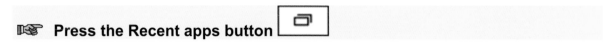 **Press the Recent apps button**

A menu with recently used apps will appear:

You may see different apps than the ones shown in this example:

☞ **For example, tap**

If you want to scroll through the list, just swipe upwards or downwards over the screen.

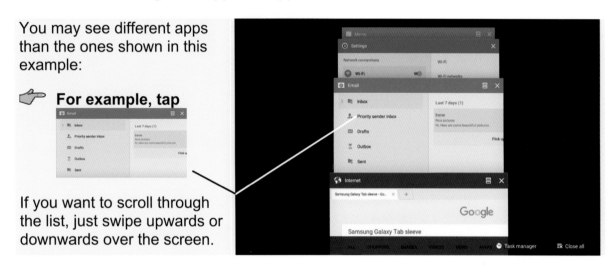

You will see the *Email* app:

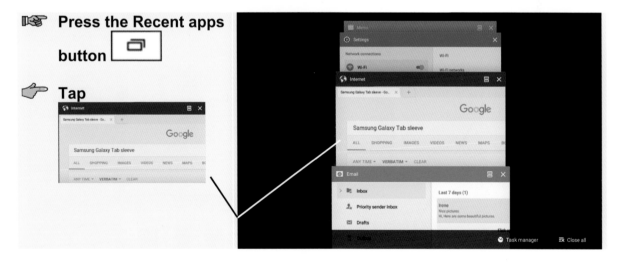

☞ **Press the Recent apps button**

☞ **Tap**

Now you will see the *Internet* app again.

You can also switch between apps using the multi window:

☞ Drag from the far right-hand side of the screen to the left

☞ Tap Email

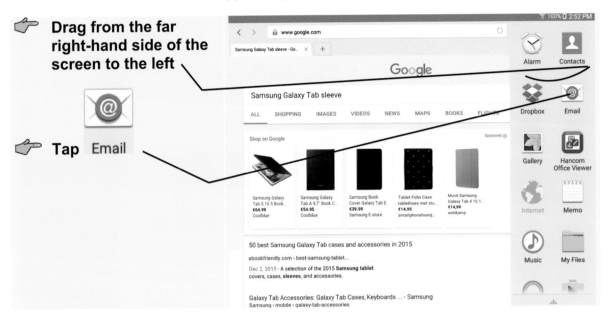

On some tablets dragging from the right-hand side does not work. You can use the multi window like this:

🖝 Press the Recent apps button [▭]

By the app you want to open:

☞ Tap ▤

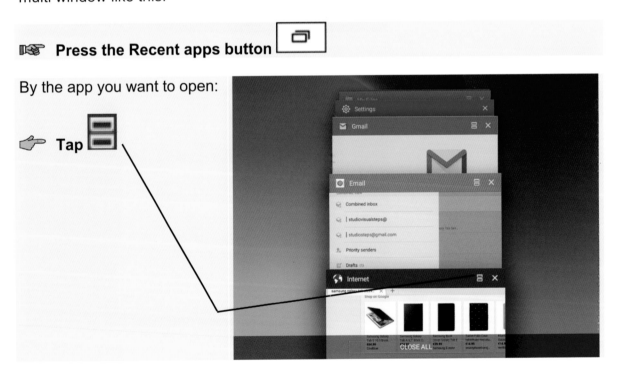

The app will be opened at the left-hand side of the screen. In this example this is the app *Internet*.

To open the *Email* app:

☞ **Tap the *Email* app**

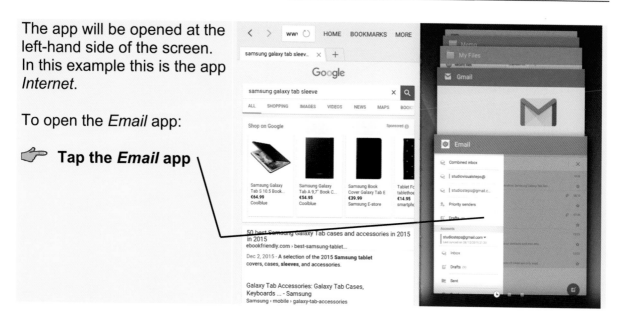

On all types of tablets:

The *Email* app has appeared on the right-hand side of the screen:

☞ **Press ◯ and hold it down**

The button will turn blue and become larger:

☞ **Drag to the left**

The panel will become larger:

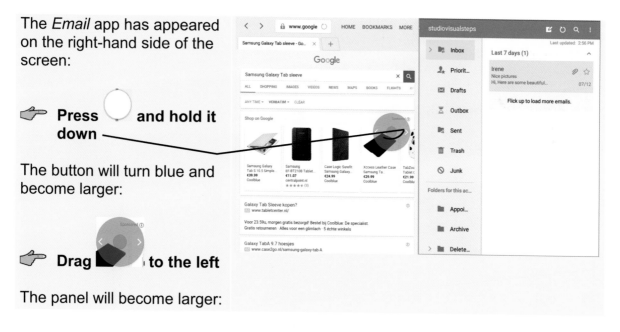

☞ **Tap**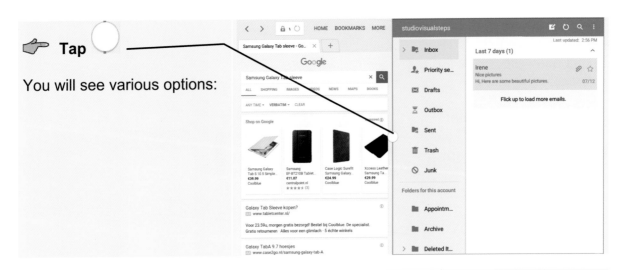

You will see various options:

Tap  to switch the position of the panel from left to right, and the other way round.

Tap to drag text, pictures or links to the other panel.

Tap to display the panel on a full screen.

Tap ✕ to close the panel.

For now, you will close the panel:

☞ **Tap** ✕

☞ **Go back to the home screen** $\mathcal{QQ}^3$

☞ **Lock or turn off the Samsung Galaxy Tab, if you wish** $\mathcal{QQ}^8$

In this chapter you have learned how to work with the *Internet* app. Furthermore, you have learned how to use new touch gestures for zooming in and out and scrolling through web pages.

3.11 Background Information

Dictionary

Bookmark	A reference to a web address stored in a list that allows quick and easy access to a web page later on.
Google	*Google* is mainly known for its search engine, but offers other services as well, such as *Google Maps* and *Gmail*.
Home page	The web page that is displayed when you open the *Internet* app, or a new tab.
Hyperlink	Another name for a link.
Link	A link is a navigation method on a web page that automatically leads the user to the information when it is tapped. It may be represented as text, an image, a button or an icon. A link is also called a hyperlink.
Scroll	Moving a web page across the screen, upwards, downwards, to the left or to the right. On the Samsung Galaxy Tab you use touch gestures to accomplish this.
Stored pages	You can store web pages in this list, and read them later on, even when you do not have an Internet connection. You can only store the page that was displayed at the time, not the entire website. If you want to view multiple web pages offline, you will need to store these pages separately.
Zoom in	Take a closer look at an item, the letters and images will be enlarged.
Zoom out	View an item from a greater distance, the letters and images will become smaller.

Source: User manual Samsung Galaxy Tab, Wikipedia

3.12 Tips

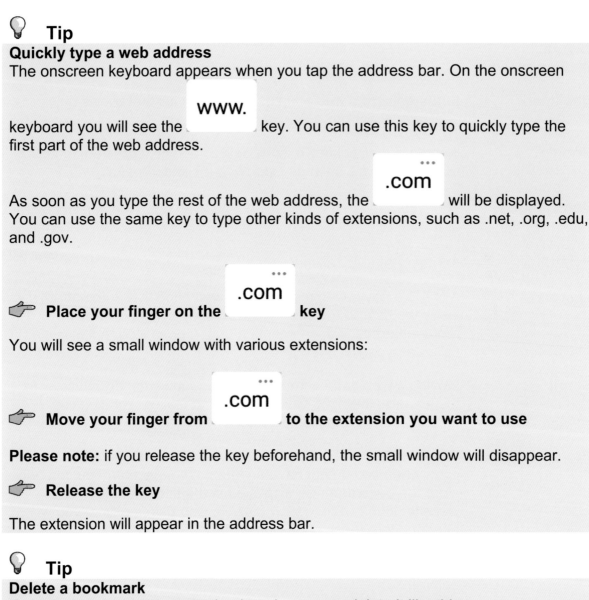

💡 **Tip**

Quickly type a web address
The onscreen keyboard appears when you tap the address bar. On the onscreen

keyboard you will see the **www.** key. You can use this key to quickly type the
first part of the web address.

As soon as you type the rest of the web address, the **.com** will be displayed.
You can use the same key to type other kinds of extensions, such as .net, .org, .edu,
and .gov.

☞ **Place your finger on the .com key**

You will see a small window with various extensions:

☞ **Move your finger from .com to the extension you want to use**

Please note: if you release the key beforehand, the small window will disappear.

☞ **Release the key**

The extension will appear in the address bar.

💡 **Tip**

Delete a bookmark
If you no longer want to use a bookmark, you can delete it like this:

☞ **Tap BOOKMARKS**

- Continue on the next page -

👉 **If necessary, drag
your finger upwards
across the screen**

👉 **Place your finger on
the bookmark you
want to delete**

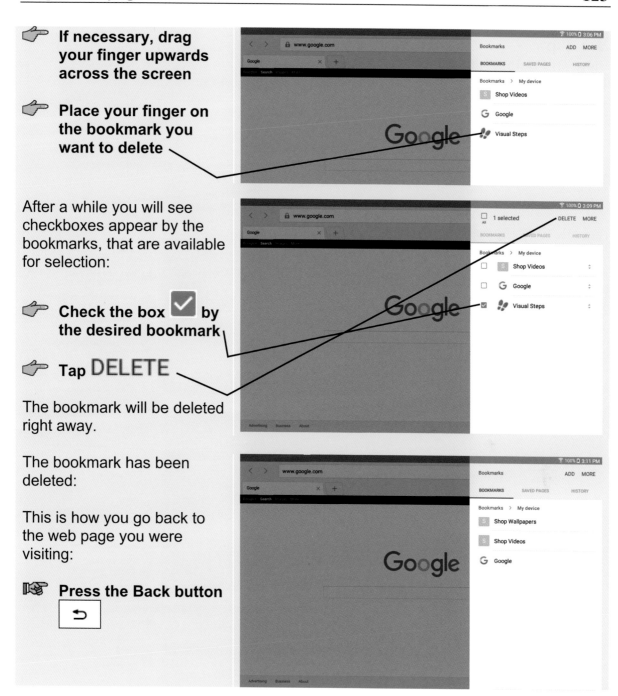

After a while you will see
checkboxes appear by the
bookmarks, that are available
for selection:

👉 **Check the box** ☑ **by
the desired bookmark**

👉 **Tap DELETE**

The bookmark will be deleted
right away.

The bookmark has been
deleted:

This is how you go back to
the web page you were
visiting:

👉 **Press the Back button
⤺**

💡 Tip

View and delete history
The browser history contains all the websites you have recently visited.
This is how you view the history:

☞ Tap BOOKMARKS

☞ Tap HISTORY

You will see the list of
recently visited pages. You
can delete this history:

☞ Tap MORE

☞ Tap Clear history

This is how you go back to
the web page you were
visiting:

☞ **Press the Back button**
↰

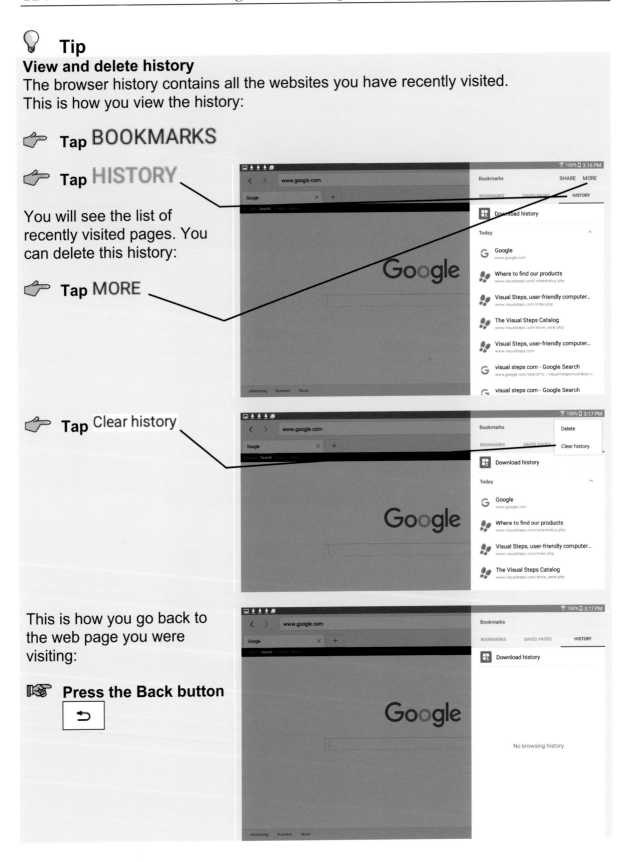

Tip

Set a home page

You can set your favorite website as the home page for your web browser. After you have opened the web page, this is what you do:

☞ **Tap** MORE

☞ **Drag upwards across the menu**

☞ **Tap** Settings

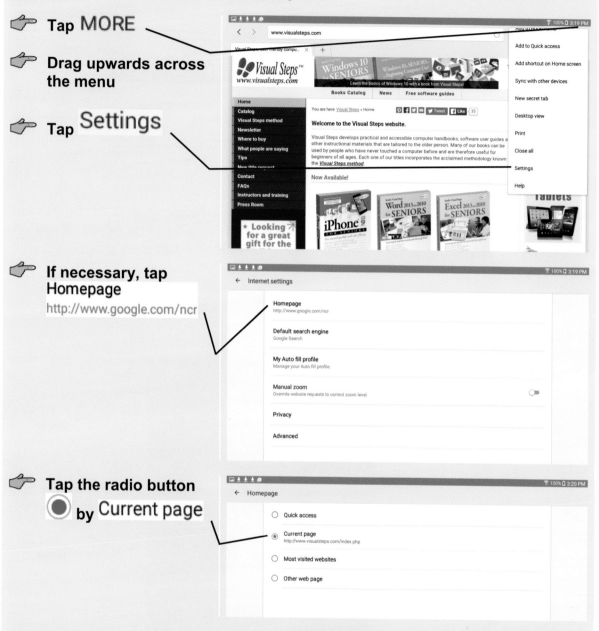

☞ **If necessary, tap Homepage**
http://www.google.com/ncr

☞ **Tap the radio button** ⦿ **by** Current page

The home page has been added. From now on, you will see your favorite website whenever you open a new tab. To save the changes:

☞ **Tap** ← Homepage, ← Internet settings

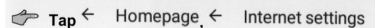

Tip

Store pages for offline reading
In the *Internet* app you can store web pages to view and read later on, for example, when you do not have a Wi-Fi connection. This is how you store a web page:

☞ Tap MORE

☞ Tap Save web page

The page will be added to the saved pages.

Please note: the page that was on the screen when you tapped the save command is the only page that will be stored, the rest of the website will not be saved. If you want to view multiple pages of a website offline, you will need to save these pages separately.

To open a web page you have previously saved:

☞ Tap BOOKMARKS

☞ Tap SAVED PAGES

☞ **Tap the desired web page**

To delete a saved page:

☞ **Place your finger on the bookmark you want to delete**

☞ **If necessary, check the box ☑ by the desired bookmark**

☞ Tap DELETE

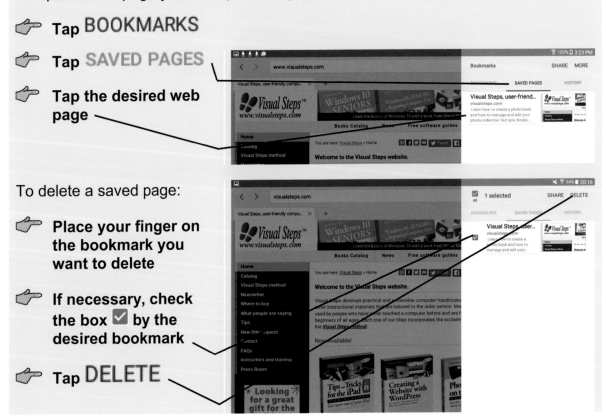

4. Managing Your Contacts, Calendar, and Widgets

Your Samsung Galaxy Tab contains a number of other standard apps besides *Email* and *Internet*. For example, you can use the *Contacts* app to manage your contacts. You can add contacts and synchronize them with the contacts list on your computer. If you choose this option, the contacts on your Tab and on your computer will become the same. You can edit or delete the contacts contained in the list directly with your Samsung Galaxy Tab.

In the *S Planner* app (also called *Calendar* app) you can keep track of your appointments and other activities. If you already keep a calendar in the *Microsoft Outlook* program, you can transfer this calendar to your Samsung Galaxy Tab. You can also add, edit, and delete events directly on the Tab.

Along with these handy apps, your tablet also features a number of standard widgets. These are small programs that offer information from the Internet or provide other useful functions. In this chapter you will find out more about them.

In this chapter you will learn how to:

- add contacts in the *Contacts* app;
- search for contacts;
- edit and delete contacts;
- add calendar items in the *S Planner* app;
- edit and delete calendar items;
- work with widgets.

 Please note:

While you are using your Tab, you may see some screens that provide additional information about the operation of an app or the keyboard. You can read the information and tap DONE or OK afterwards.

4.1 Adding a Contact

Open the *Contacts* app from the list of all apps, or from the home screen:

☞ **Turn on** 𝒪𝒪⁴ **or unlock the Samsung Galaxy Tab** 𝒪𝒪⁹

👉 **If necessary, tap** 🔲

👉 **Tap** Contacts

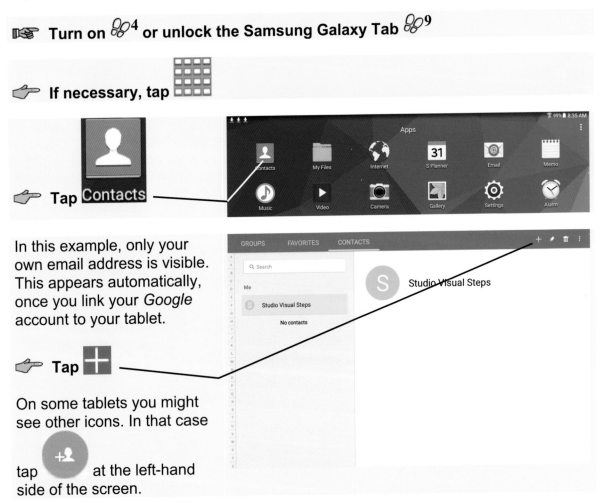

In this example, only your own email address is visible. This appears automatically, once you link your *Google* account to your tablet.

👉 **Tap** ➕

On some tablets you might see other icons. In that case

tap 🔘 at the left-hand side of the screen.

You might be asked where you want to save the new contact. You can choose between the SIM card (on the Samsung Galaxy Tab Wi-Fi + 3G/4G), your *Google* account, your Samsung account, or on this device only. In this example the *Google* account will be chosen. In this way you can automatically synchronize your contacts with your computer and other devices, if you wish.

👉 **Tap**
   G **Google**

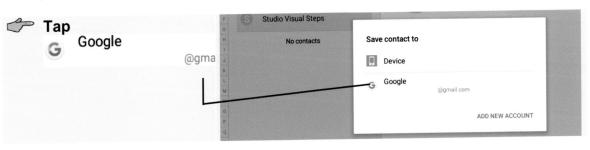

You may see this message:

 If necessary, tap OK

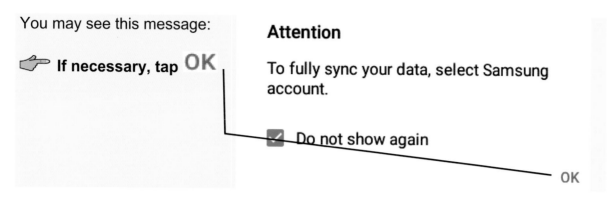

Attention

To fully sync your data, select Samsung account.

☑ Do not show again

OK

💡 **Tip**

Contacts will be synchronized
If you have already added contacts to your *Google* account on another device, such as a cell phone, they will be synchronized automatically to your Samsung Galaxy Tab when you are connected to the Internet.

You will see the window where you can add a new contact:

By Name, tap ⌄

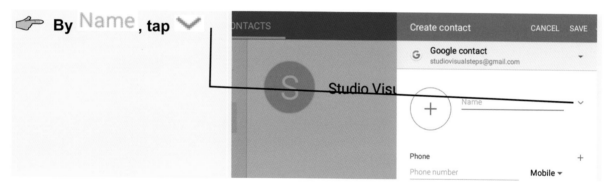

In this example we will add a fictitious contact. You can type the actual data for a friend or family member, if you wish. You do this by using the onscreen keyboard:

Tap First name

⌨ **Type your contact's first name**

Tap Last name

⌨ **Type your contact's last name**

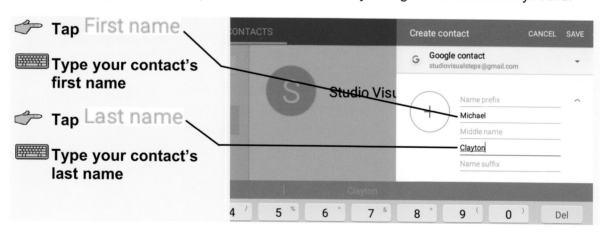

You can choose which fields you want to fill in. You also can reduce the size of the name box like this:

 **Tap** ︿

💡   **Tip**
Even faster
If you only use the First name and Last name boxes, you really do not need to open the box. You can just type the full name (for example: Michael Clayton) directly into the Name box.

☞ **Tap** Phone number

⌨ **Type your contact's mobile phone number**

Add a second line for a phone number:

☞ **Tap** ✚

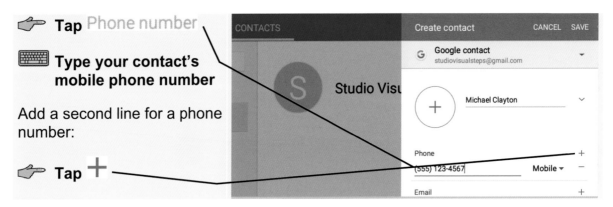

🢂**Please note:**
If you type a phone number, sometimes blank spaces will be added automatically and sometimes they will not. But when you need to use the phone number it doesn't matter if there are blank spaces or not.

By default, the label for the next phone number field is **Work** ▾. You can change this label yourself. You can turn it into a home phone number, for instance:

☞ **Tap** Work ▾

If you see another name on the label, then tap that label.

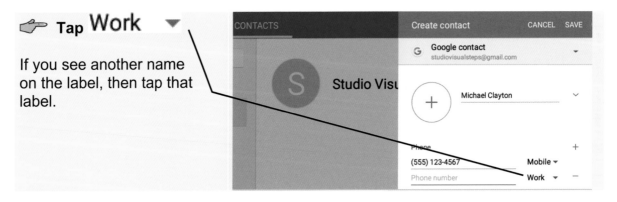

You will see a list of available labels:

☞ **Tap** Home

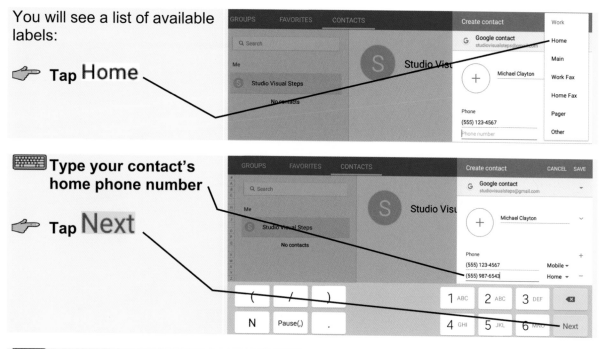

⌨ **Type your contact's home phone number**

☞ **Tap** Next

⌨ **Type your contact's email address**

💡 **Tip**

Change the label
You can also change the label for an email address, from home to work, for example.

On the keyboard:

☞ **Tap** Done

Now you can add your contact's home address. You will need to add a field first:

☞ **If necessary, drag the page upwards**

☞ **Tap**

ADD ANOTHER FIELD

In the next window:

☞ **Check the box ✅ by Address**

☞ **Tap OK or ADD**

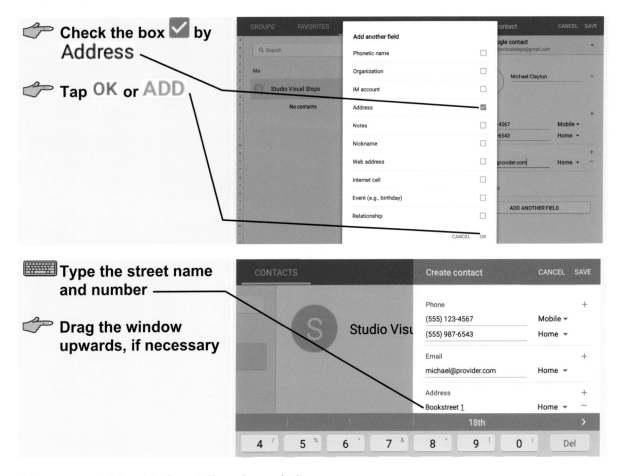

⌨ **Type the street name and number**

☞ **Drag the window upwards, if necessary**

Now you add the zip (postal) code and city:

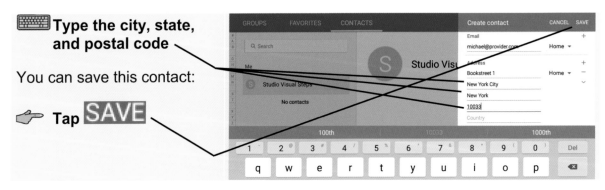

⌨ **Type the city, state, and postal code**

You can save this contact:

☞ **Tap SAVE**

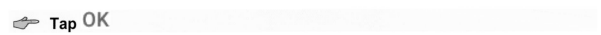

You will see a message about your contact having multiple phone numbers. You can select one of these numbers as the default phone number:

☞ **Tap OK**

☞ **If necessary, tap the radio button ◉ by the number you want to set as a default**

☞ **Tap** `DONE`

If you do not see this option, it is not available on your tablet.

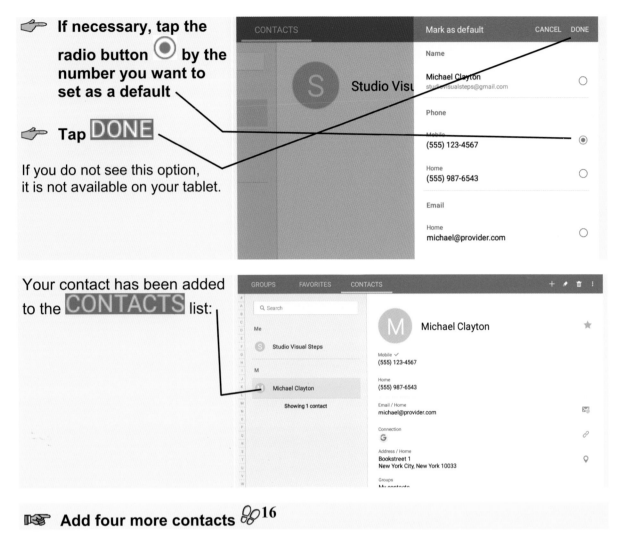

Your contact has been added to the `CONTACTS` list:

☞ **Add four more contacts** ⠧16

You may have some difficulty reading all the names in your contact list. If you widen the name box a little, it is easier to read the full names:

☞ **Place your finger on the borderline between the list and the contact data**

The borderline will be more visible:

☞ **Drag to the right**

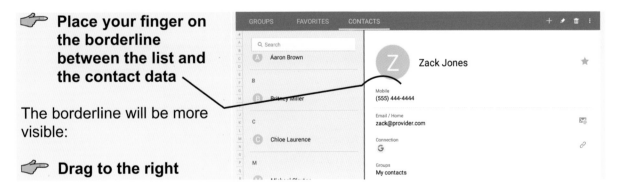

Now you can read even the longer names. If you want to make the box a bit smaller again, just drag the line a little to the left.

4.2 Editing a Contact

After you have added all your contacts, you may want to edit the data later on. For example, in order to change an address, or add a new phone number. This is how you open a contact for editing:

☞ **Tap the desired contact**

☞ **Tap ✎ or EDIT**

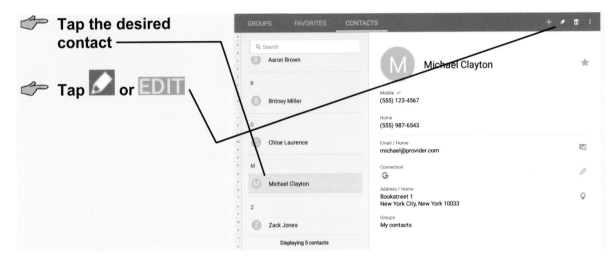

This is how you edit the phone number, for example:

☞ **Place your finger on the phone number**

The phone number is selected:

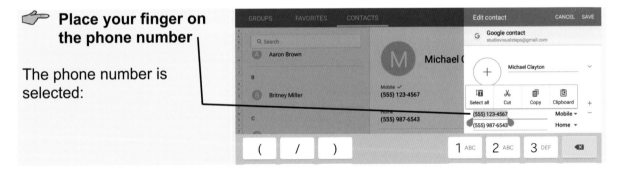

You can type the new phone number right away:

⌨ **Type the new phone number**

☞ **Tap SAVE**

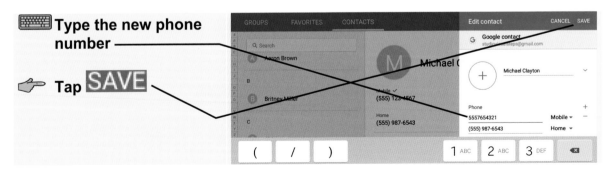

4.3 Finding a Contact

If you have added a lot of contacts to the *Contacts* app, it may be difficult to quickly find the right contact. Fortunately, the app contains a handy search function:

☞ **Tap** $\mathcal{Q}$ **Search**

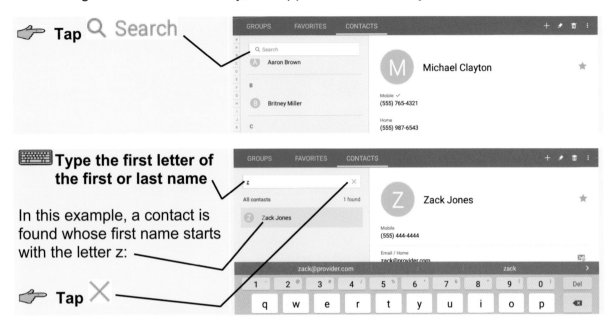

⌨ **Type the first letter of the first or last name**

In this example, a contact is found whose first name starts with the letter z:

☞ **Tap** ✕

4.4 Deleting a Contact

This is how you delete unnecessary contacts:

☞ **Tap the desired contact**

☞ **Tap** 🗑

On some tablets you will not see the 🗑 icon. Then you delete a contact like this:

☞ **Tap MORE**

☞ **Tap Delete**

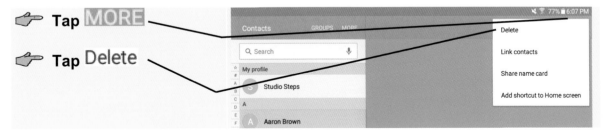

You will need to confirm this action:

👉 **Tap OK or DELETE**

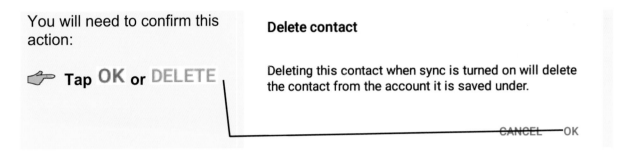

Delete contact

Deleting this contact when sync is turned on will delete the contact from the account it is saved under.

CANCEL   OK

☞ **Go back to the home screen** 👣³

4.5 S Planner

In the *S Planner* you can keep a diary. This is how you open the app:

👉 **If necessary, tap** ⬜⬜⬜⬜

👉 **Tap S Planner**

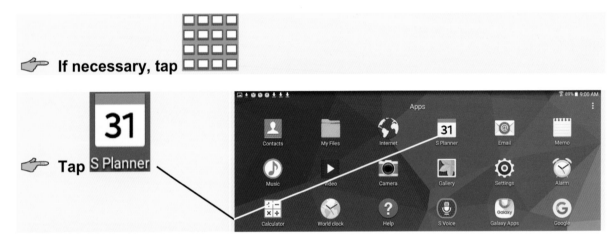

The calendar opens with a view of the current month:

At the top you can select a different view:

If you have selected another date than the current day, you can use the **TODAY** button to quickly return to today's events:

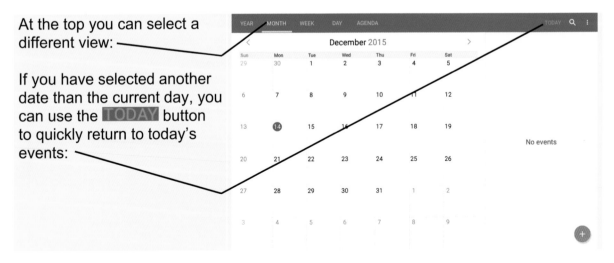

You can change the view per day, week, month, and year. You can view a full week at once, for example:

☞ Tap WEEK

You will see this week's view. You can quickly jump to the next week:

☞ **Swipe over the screen from right to left**

You will see the next week.

4.6 Adding an Event to the Calendar

An appointment is called an event in the *S Planner* app. You can practice adding an event to your calendar:

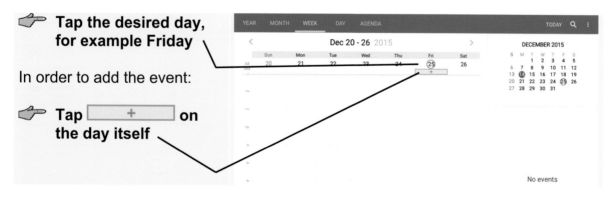

☞ **Tap the desired day, for example Friday**

In order to add the event:

☞ **Tap** ___+___ **on the day itself**

You may see a message regarding synchronization. Your *Google* calendar will automatically be synchronized with your *Google* account. For now you do not need to change any of these settings.

☞ **If necessary, tap** OK

You can enter a name for the event:

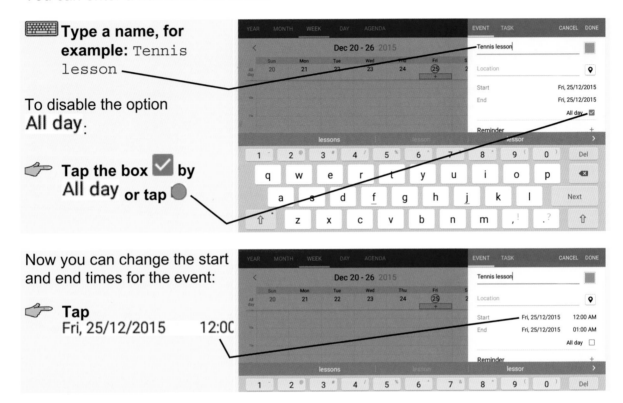

⌨ **Type a name, for example:** Tennis lesson

To disable the option **All day**:

☞ **Tap the box** ☑ **by All day or tap** ⬤

Now you can change the start and end times for the event:

☞ **Tap** Fri, 25/12/2015 12:00

You can adjust the hours and minutes forward or backward with the ⌃ and ⌄ buttons:

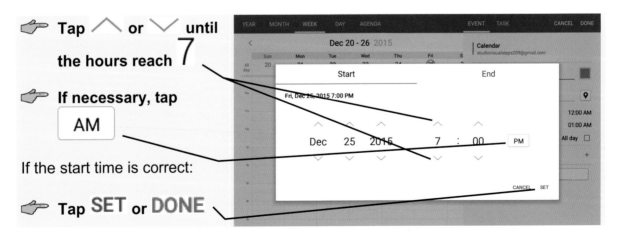

☞ **Tap** ⌃ **or** ⌄ **until the hours reach** 7

☞ **If necessary, tap** AM

If the start time is correct:

☞ **Tap** SET **or** DONE

The end time is automatically adjusted to 8:00 PM:

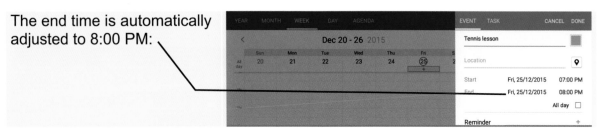

 Tip

Correct start time

If you add an event by clicking the correct time box at the beginning, the start time will be set correctly right away.

Tip

Whole day

If an event lasts all day. By **All day**:

👉 **Check the box** ✅

Or:

👉 **Tap** ⬡

You can also use the Reminder option in the window where you add an event:

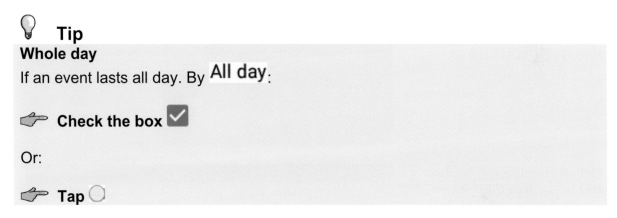

Reminder or ⏰ : Here you can set a reminder for the activity by tapping ➕ . The reminder will be sent in the form of a notification or an email. You can choose whether you want to be reminded just a couple of minutes before the event starts, or even a couple of hours, or days. By default, the **Notification** and **15 min before** options have been selected.

You can use even more options in the window where you add an event. On some tablets you might need to tap │ **VIEW MORE OPTIONS** │ first to see the options. Here are two examples of the options:

Privacy : Here you change the privacy settings. You can choose Default, Private and public.

Repeat : Here you can set the event to be repeated with a certain frequency. For instance, every week or every month. By default, the One-time event option has been selected.

You can also enter a location for the event:

☞ **Tap** Location

⌨ **Type a location, for example:** Tennis court

After you have entered all the data concerning the event:

☞ **Tap** DONE **or** SAVE

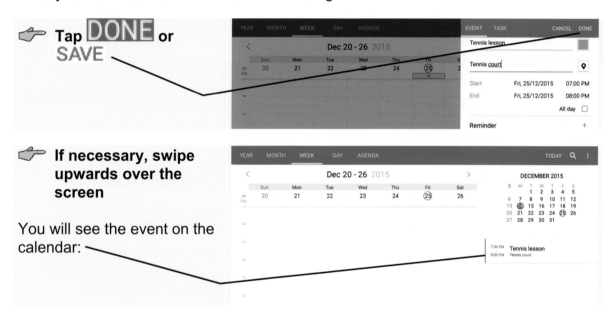

☞ **If necessary, swipe upwards over the screen**

You will see the event on the calendar:

4.7 Editing or Deleting an Event

If an event changes or is canceled, you can edit it like this:

☞ **Tap the event**

☞ **Tap** ✏ **or** EDIT

You may see a message about the *Google* calendar not being able to synchronize:

☞ **If necessary, tap** OK

You will see the window again where you had entered the event. For now you do not need to change anything:

☞ **Tap** CANCEL

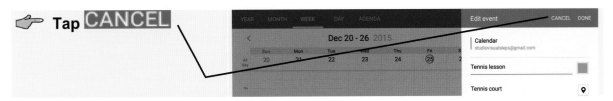

If you want to delete the event, you can do that like this:

☞ **Tap the event**

☞ **If necessary, tap**

☞ **Tap** Delete

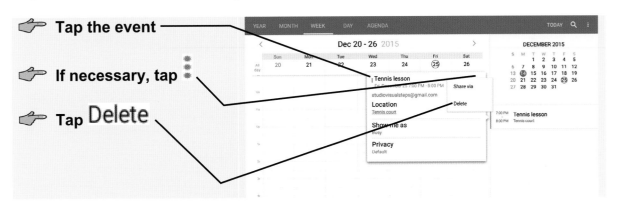

You will need to confirm this action:

☞ **Tap** DELETE

☞ **Go back to the home screen** 𝒦𝒦³

4.8 Working with Widgets

The home screen of your tablet contains one or a number of *widgets*. These are small programs that offer information from the Internet or provide other useful functions. On your other pages, you may see some widgets too, for example, the second or third page:

☞ **Drag the screen from right to left**

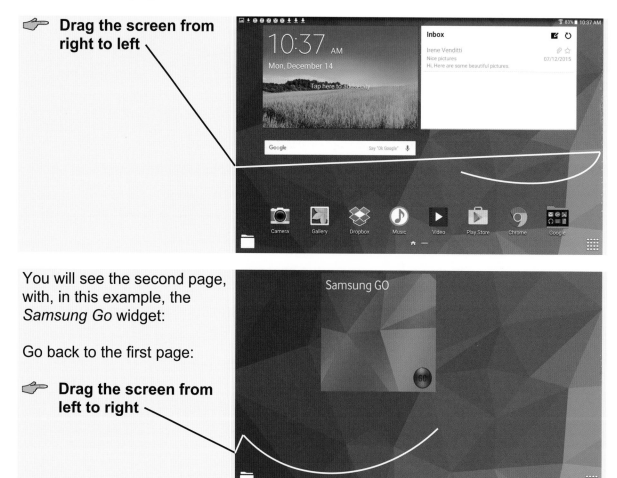

You will see the second page, with, in this example, the *Samsung Go* widget:

Go back to the first page:

☞ **Drag the screen from left to right**

This is how you use the weather widget, for example:

☞ **Tap**
Tap here to add a city

On some tablets the home screen looks like this:

You can start the weather widget like this:

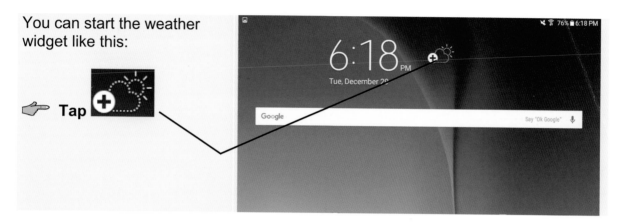

☞ **Tap** ⊕

You might see a message about the use of your current location:

☞ **Tap the desired option**

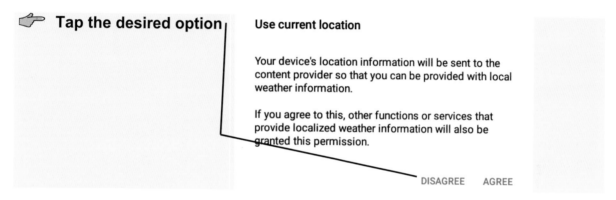

Use current location

Your device's location information will be sent to the content provider so that you can be provided with local weather information.

If you agree to this, other functions or services that provide localized weather information will also be granted this permission.

DISAGREE   AGREE

The program will probably want to search for your location:

☞ **Tap your current location**

New York
New York, United States

If you do not see your current location or if you want to add a different location:

⌨ **Type the location**

☞ **Tap the location**

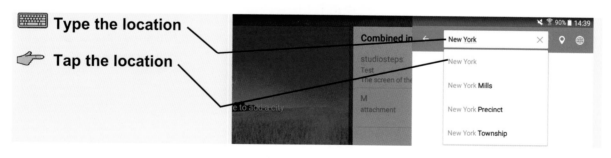

☞ **If necessary, tap the location again**

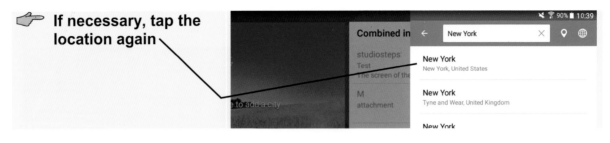

🖙 **If necessary, go back to the home screen** 👣³

You will see the widget with the current weather forecast appear on your home screen:

On some tablets you will see a smaller widget

on the home screen.

There are several other widgets you can use. Here is how to view them:

☞ **Press your finger to the home screen**

☞ **Tap** Widgets

Now you will see a screen with various widgets.

To view more widgets:

☞ **Swipe the screen from right to left**

In this example we select the widget *S Planner*. This widget has multiple views. You can see that there are multiple views by :

☞ **Tap the widget**

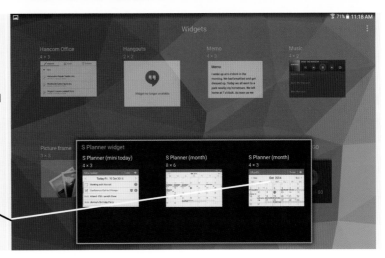

In this example, the *S Planner (month) 4 x 3* widget is selected. You may not see this widget on your own screen. If that is the case, you can select a different widget.

☞ **Place your finger on the widget**

The Tab suggests placing the app on the first page, but this page is already quite crowded. You can place the widget on the second page:

☞ **Drag to the right-hand edge of the screen**

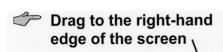

Now, you can place the widget on the second page:

☞ **Release the widget**

The widget has been placed on the second page:

If you have selected the *S Planner* widget, you will see today's date: ————

If an event has been added, you will see it in the widget:

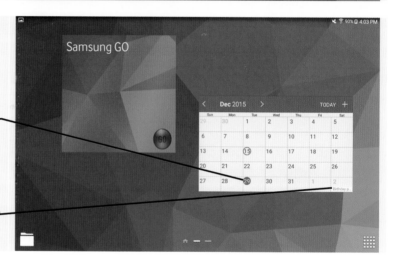

You can also drag a widget to another page:

☞ **Place your finger on the widget**

☞ **Drag to the right-hand edge of the screen**

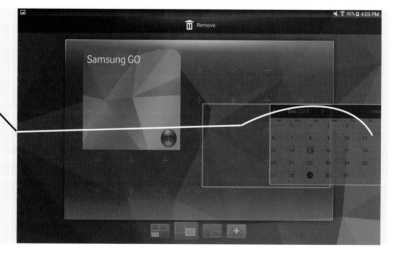

☞ **Release the widget**

☞ **Place one more widget on the page that is displayed** 👣³⁰

This is how you delete a widget if you do not want it to be displayed on the page anymore:

👉 **Place your finger on the widget**

👉 **Drag to** 🗑

👉 **Release the widget**

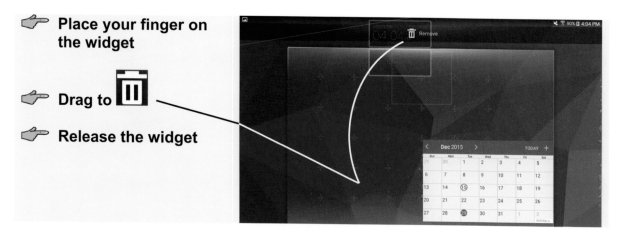

The widget has been removed from the page.

☞ **Go back to the home screen** 👣³

☞ **Lock or turn off the Samsung Galaxy Tab, if you wish** 👣⁸

In this chapter you have learned to use the *Contacts* and *S Planner* apps. You have also learned how to work with widgets.

4.9 Background Information

Dictionary

Contacts	An app in which you can add and manage contacts.
Event	An appointment in the *S Planner* app.
Field	The box where you enter data for a contact. *First name* and *Postal code* are examples of fields.
Google Calendar	A service offered by *Google*, where you can keep a calendar. You can use your *Google* account for this.
Hangouts	An app with which you can hold video chats through an Internet connection. You can chat with friends who have a *Google* account and use *Google Hangouts* as well.
Label	Name of a field.
Outlook	An email program, part of the *Microsoft Office* suite.
S Planner	An app with which you can keep track of your activities and appointments.
Synchronize	Literally, this means equalizing. When you synchronize your Tab with *Smart Switch*, the content will be placed in a folder on your computer.

Source: User manual Samsung Galaxy Tab, Wikipedia

4.10 Tips

 Tip

Add a photo

If you have stored a photo of your contact on your tablet, you can add this photo to his or her contact information. In *Chapter 7 Photos and Video* you can read how to take pictures with your tablet and how to transfer photos to your tablet. This is how you add an existing photo to a contact:

☞ **Open the *Contacts* app** &⃝17

☞ **Tap the desired contact**

☞ **Tap** 🖊 **or** EDIT

☞ **Tap** or

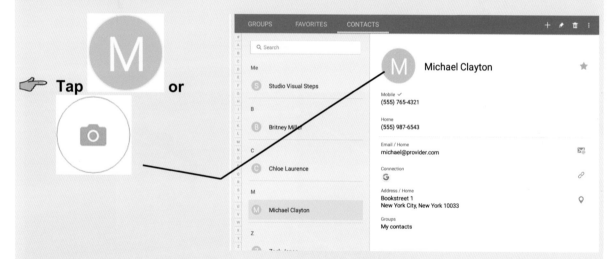

☞ **Tap** Images

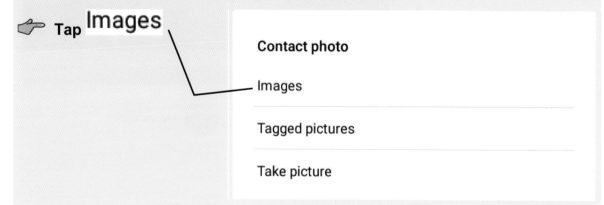

- Continue on the next page -

You might need to select the photo album that contains the photo:

☞ **If necessary, tap the desired album**

☞ **Tap the desired photo**

☞ **If necessary, tap**

Crop picture

☞ **If necessary, tap JUST ONCE**

Complete action using

Crop picture   Crop photo

JUST ONCE   ALWAYS

If you wish, you can use the handles ◯ to change the position of the blue frame:

The part of the photo that lies within the frame is the part that will be used.

☞ **Tap DONE**

The photo has been added to the contact data:

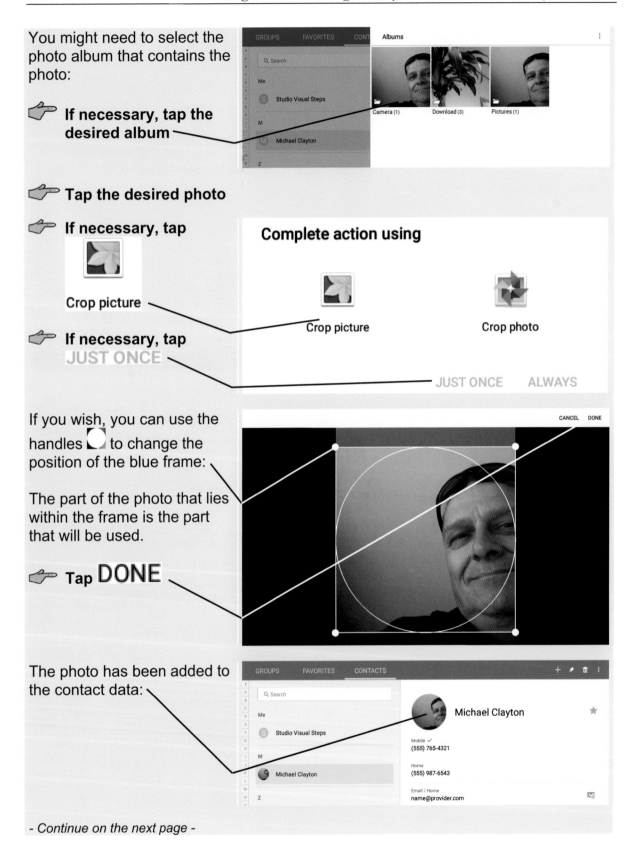

Michael Clayton

Mobile ✓
(555) 765-4321

Home
(555) 987-6543

Email / Home
name@provider.com

- Continue on the next page -

On some tablets you will need to save this change:

☞ **If necessary, tap**

💡 **Tip**
Delete a field
In *section 4.1 Adding a Contact* you have seen how you can add a new field. This is how you delete the field:

☞ **By the desired field, tap** ▬

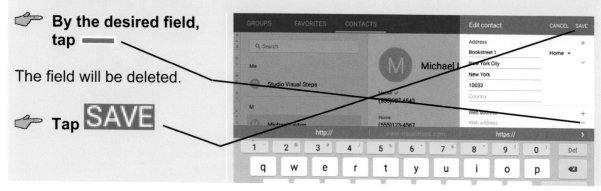

The field will be deleted.

☞ **Tap**

💡 **Tip**
Synchronize contacts
The contacts you have saved in your *Google* account will automatically be synchronized with all the devices on which you use this *Google* account. If you already use a different program on your computer for managing your contacts, you may be able to synchronize the contact data with your Samsung Galaxy Tab. Currently, this is only possible with your *Microsoft Office Outlook* contacts.

On your computer:

☞ **Open *Smart Switch*** 11

☞ **Connect your Samsung Galaxy Tab to the computer**

- Continue on the next page -

At the bottom of the window:

☞ **Click**

At the bottom of the window:

☞ **Click**
Sync Preferences for Outlook

In order to copy contacts from *Outlook* to your tablet:

☞ **Check the box ☐ by**
Contacts

☞ **By** Apply to both device and
Outlook ⌄ , **click** ☟

☞ **Click** Apply to device only

In this example, all the
contacts will be
synchronized:

☞ **Click** OK

On the next screen:

☞ **Click** Sync Now

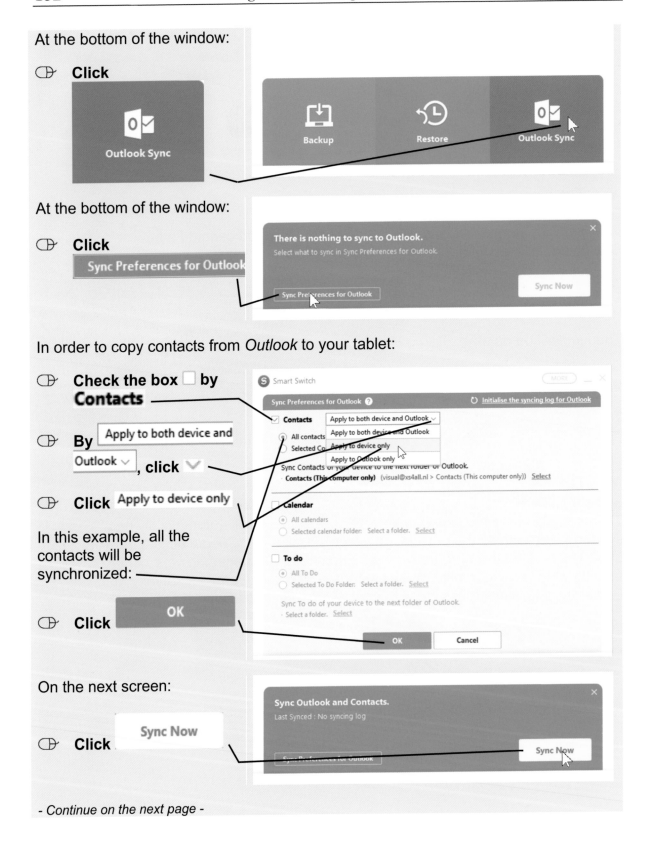

- Continue on the next page -

The contacts are synchronized:

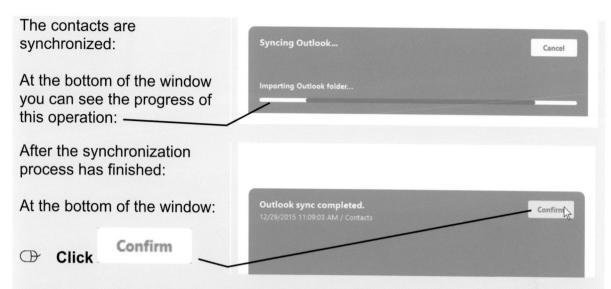

At the bottom of the window you can see the progress of this operation:

After the synchronization process has finished:

At the bottom of the window:

⊕ **Click** Confirm

Now the contacts have also been copied to the *Contacts* app on your tablet. Because you have saved the contacts you added on your tablet in your *Google* account, these contacts have not been saved in *Outlook*. But this is not necessary, since you have saved these contacts online, so you can access them on different devices.

☞ **Close** *Smart Switch* ℘⁷

☞ **Safely disconnect the Samsung Galaxy Tab from the computer**

☞ **Open the** *Contacts* **app** ℘17

The new contacts have been added. They have not been saved in your *Google* account. This is how you solve this problem. On some tablets you will see the option MORE at the left-hand side of the screen of the app *Contacts*. If you see this option, then use the information on the next page.

👉 **Tap the contact**

Here you can see that the contact is saved to the device:

👉 **Tap** ⦙

👉 **Tap** Move device contacts to

- Continue on the next page -

☞ **Tap** Google

Now all contacts have been saved in your *Google* account.

Move device contacts to

Google

Samsung account

If you see the option MORE you can save the contacts to your *Google* account like this:

☞ **Tap** MORE

☞ **Tap** Settings

☞ **Tap**
Move device contacts

☞ **Tap** Google

Now all contacts have been saved in your *Google* account.

Move device contacts to

Google

Samsung account

Tip

Synchronize your calendar with Outlook

If you keep your calendar on your computer in *Outlook*, you can synchronize this calendar with your Tab. Then the calendar events from *Outlook* will be added to the *S Planner* app. But you will still be able to simultaneously view the items in the *S Planner* app. The events from your tablet will not be added to your *Outlook* calendar. On your computer:

☞ **Open *Smart Switch*** ✌11

☞ **Connect your tablet to the computer**

☞ **Click** Outlook Sync

☞ **Click** Sync Preferences for Outlook

☞ **Check the box** ☑ **by** **Calendar**

By default, all the items in the calendar will be synchronized:

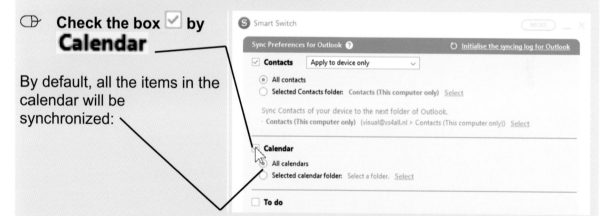

If you want to synchronize a specific folder with calendar items, you need to click the radio button ⃝ by **Selected calendar folder:**. Next, you click Select, and you check the box ☑ by the desired option(s), then you click **OK**.

- Continue on the next page -

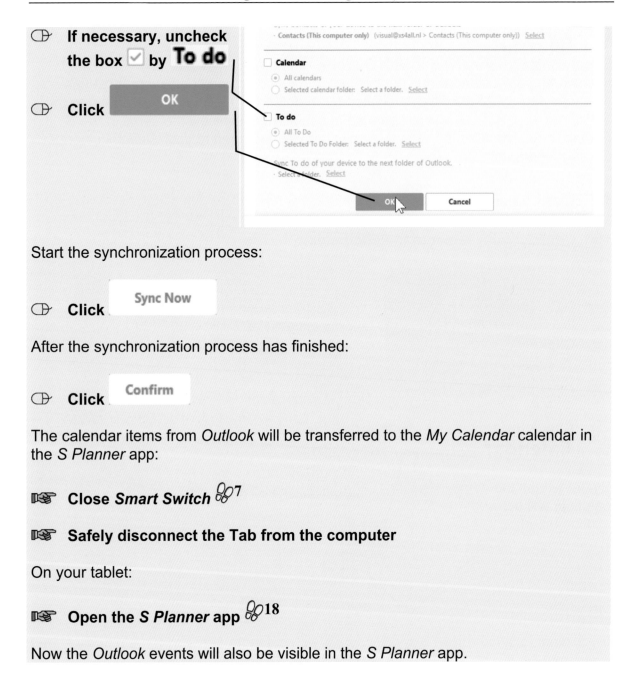

☞ **If necessary, uncheck the box** ☑ **by To do**

☞ **Click** OK

Start the synchronization process:

☞ **Click** Sync Now

After the synchronization process has finished:

☞ **Click** Confirm

The calendar items from *Outlook* will be transferred to the *My Calendar* calendar in the *S Planner* app:

☞ **Close *Smart Switch*** ✂️[7]

☞ **Safely disconnect the Tab from the computer**

On your tablet:

☞ **Open the *S Planner* app** ✂️[18]

Now the *Outlook* events will also be visible in the *S Planner* app.

5. Maps, Google Search, and Managing Files

In the *Maps* app you can look up addresses and well-known locations. You can view these locations on a regular map and on a satellite photo as well. Many locations allow you to use the *Google Street View* function. This makes it look as if you are actually there, on the spot. Once you have found the desired location, you can get directions on how to get there.

Google Search is the search function on your Samsung Galaxy Tab. This function enables you to search all the apps, contacts, messages, and music stored on your Samsung Galaxy Tab. If you are connected to the Internet you can also use this function to search the Internet.

Furthermore, you can also manage files on your tablet. For example, files or photos you have downloaded from the Internet. You can find these files with the *My Files* app. You can place these files in a specific folder, or delete them, among other things.

In this chapter, you will learn more about these useful apps. You will also learn how to close an app or turn it off.

In this chapter you will learn how to:

- determine your present location in the *Maps* app;
- view a satellite photo;
- find and view a location with *Street View*;
- get directions;
- search with the *Google Search* app;
- work with the *My Files* app;
- close apps.

 Please note:

While you are using your Tab, you may see some screens that provide additional information about the operation of an app or the keyboard. You can read the information and tap **DONE** or **OK** afterwards.

5.1 Maps

You can use the *Maps* app to find a location and get directions for a future journey. You do need to have an Internet connection established in order to use this function. This is how you open the *Maps* app:

☞ **Turn on** 👣⁴ **or unlock the Samsung Galaxy Tab** 👣⁹

☞ **If necessary, tap** ⊞

☞ **Tap Maps**

You may see this welcome message:

☞ **If necessary, tap**

ACCEPT & CONTINUE

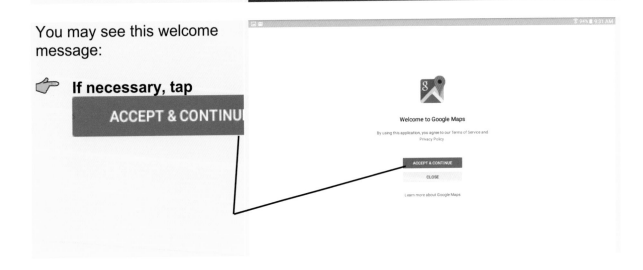

In the next screen you will be asked whether or not you would like to allow *Google* to use your location information. In the example this option is chosen:

 Tap

YES, I'M IN

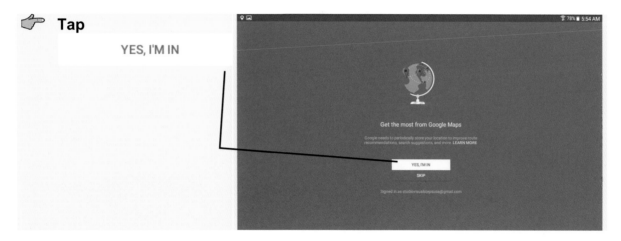

You will see a map of your country:

Of course, you will see a different location from the one used in this example.

You can change the view of the map by adding layers:

 Tap ≡

 Please note:

You may see a screen regarding tips for improving the accuracy of your location. To improve the accuracy:

 Tap Settings

- Continue on the next page -

☞ **Tap** Mode

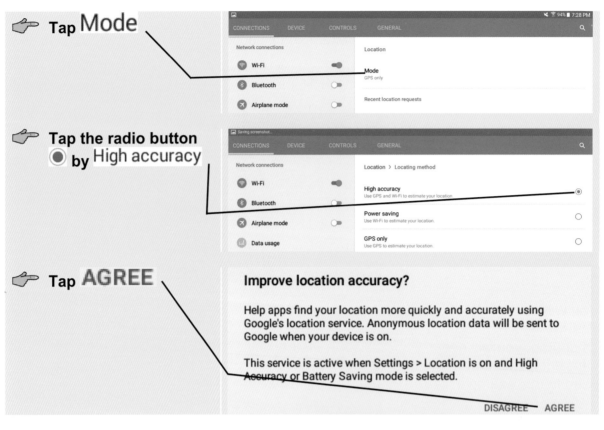

☞ **Tap the radio button**
    ⦿ **by** High accuracy

☞ **Tap** AGREE

Improve location accuracy?

Help apps find your location more quickly and accurately using Google's location service. Anonymous location data will be sent to Google when your device is on.

This service is active when Settings > Location is on and High Accuracy or Battery Saving mode is selected.

DISAGREE   AGREE

You can select various options:

☞ **Tap** 🖼   **Satellite**

You will see a satellite photo of your current location:

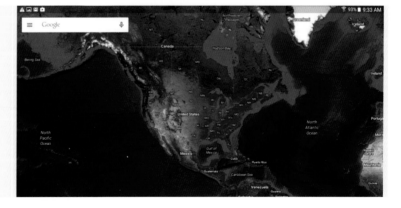

5.2 Searching for a Location with Street View

There are times when you want to find a certain location. If you have an address available you can search for it directly in *Maps*. You can also look for well-known public places or a city's local attractions:

☞ **Tap**
Search Google Maps

⌨ **Type:** Guggenheim
Museum

☞ **Tap** Q

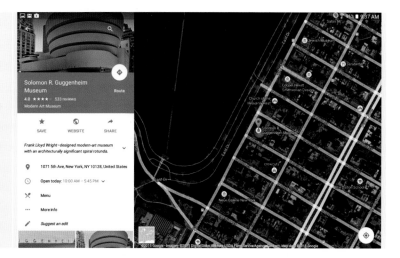

The location is represented by an icon: .

Zoom in on the location:

☞ **Spread two fingers across the map**

💡 **Tip**

Zoom out
Move two fingers towards one another (pinch) in order to zoom out.

☞　**Tap the screen**

You will see that the pane with information on the left-hand side disappears:

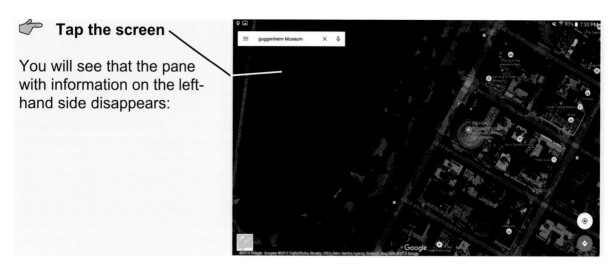

Once you have found a location in *Maps*, you can look at it more closely using the *Street View* function:

☞　**Tap**

The location information will be shown again.

In the pane on the left-hand side:

☞　**Drag the pane upwards**

☞　**Tap the photo containing the Street View text**

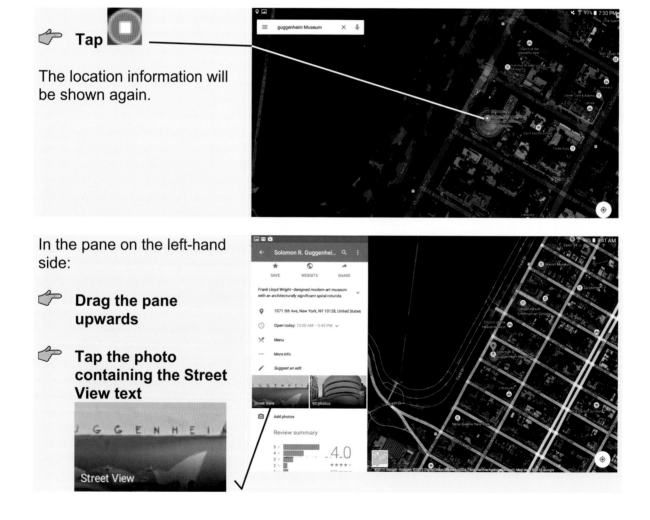

The location will be opened in *Google Street View*:

You will find yourself in front of the museum. In order to view the top of the museum:

 Drag the screen from top to bottom

You will see the image moving upwards:

You can also take a look at the surroundings:

 Drag the screen from bottom to top

 Drag the screen from right to left

You will be looking down the street:

By using the 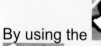 and

 arrows you can move to a different spot:

 Tap the top arrow

three times

You will proceed further down the street:

If you want to go back to the map view:

☞ **Press the Back key**

↰

5.3 Getting Directions

Now you are back in the Map view. Once you have found the desired location, you can get directions to it, like this:

☞ **Drag the pane downwards**

☞ **Tap** Route

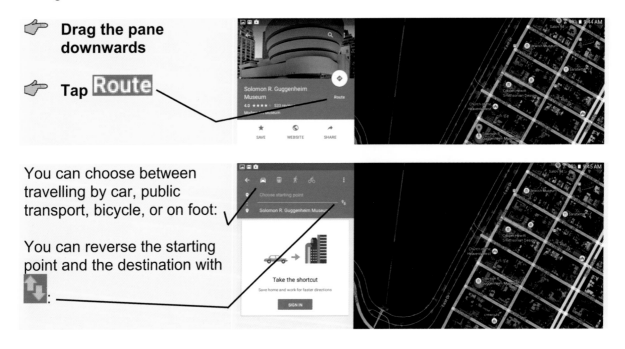

You can choose between travelling by car, public transport, bicycle, or on foot:

You can reverse the starting point and the destination with ⬆⬇ :

Enter a new starting point:

By Choose starting point:

Type: Empire Hotel

☞ **Tap**

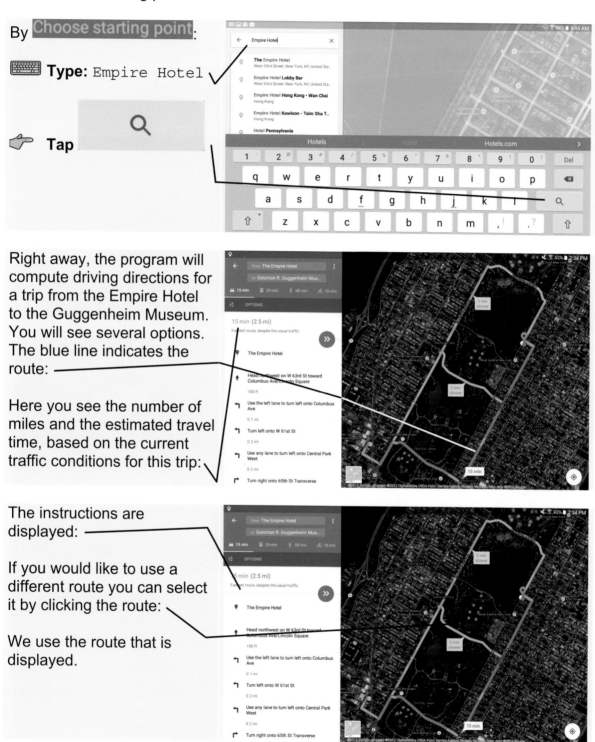

Right away, the program will compute driving directions for a trip from the Empire Hotel to the Guggenheim Museum. You will see several options. The blue line indicates the route:

Here you see the number of miles and the estimated travel time, based on the current traffic conditions for this trip:

The instructions are displayed:

If you would like to use a different route you can select it by clicking the route:

We use the route that is displayed.

By tapping the instructions you can display parts of the route:

☞ **Tap** ↰   **Use any lane to turn left onto Central Park West**

You will see part of the route:

You can follow the route step by step, by constantly tapping

〉 . For now, this will not be necessary.

☞ **Press the Back key**
⤺

☞ **Tap** ⬅

You can make the pane with information disappear:

☞ **Tap the map**

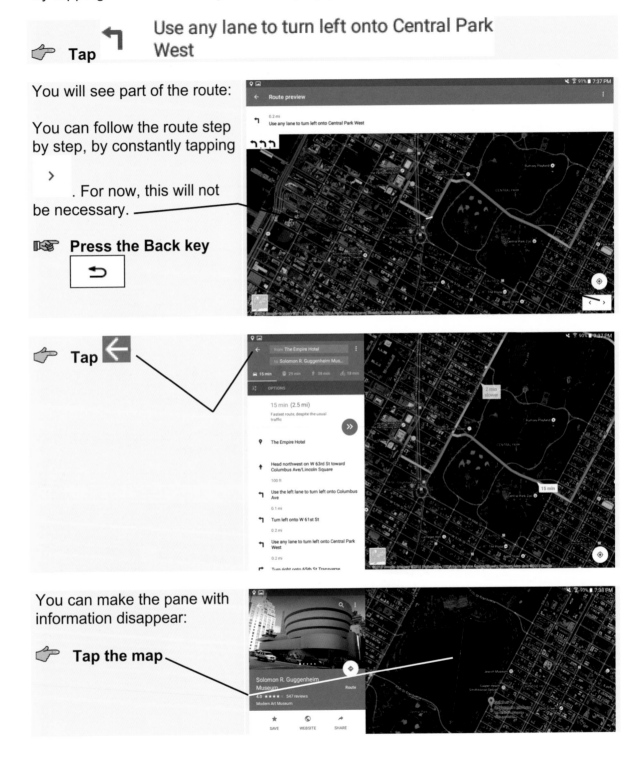

The pane disappears. You can return to your current location, like this:

In the bottom right-hand corner of the screen:

☞ **Tap**

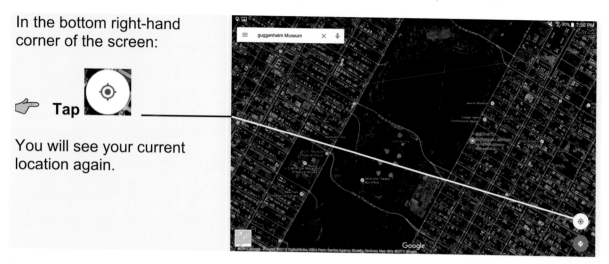

You will see your current location again.

▶ **Go back to the home screen** 👣³

5.4 Searching

Google Search is the app that provides search functionality for your Samsung Galaxy Tab. Here is how you open *Google Search*:

☞ **Tap** Google

First, you will see some information about *Google Now*:

You might see a slightly
different screen. This screen
can change regularly:

☞ **Tap** SKIP

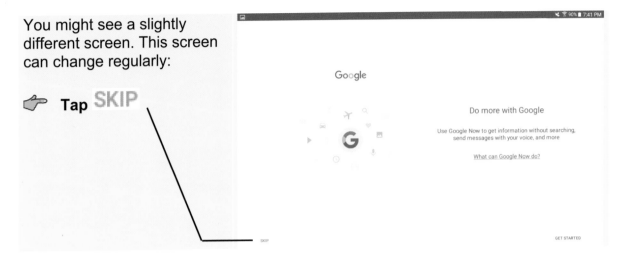

If Wi-Fi and the mobile data network (if applicable) have been turned off, the *Google Search* app will search the content of your tablet only. If an Internet connection has been enabled, the Internet will be searched as well.

In this example we are going to see which items are found beginning with the letter m:

⌨ **Type:** m

You will see the Internet
search suggestions for words
that begin with the letter m:

Below there are various apps
that begin with an m:

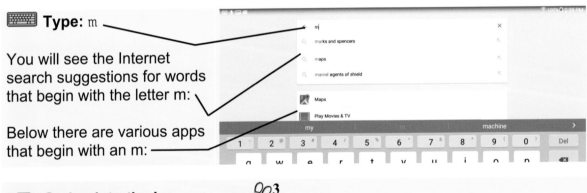

☞ **Go back to the home screen** 👣³

💡 **Tip**
Open *Google Search* from the apps list
You can also open the *Google Search* app using the apps list:

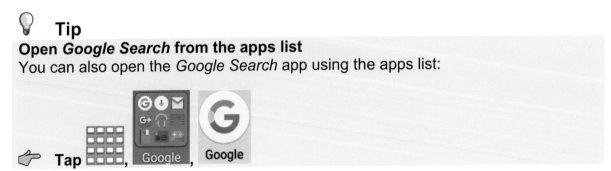

☞ **Tap** ⬛, Google , **Google**

5.5 The My Files App

When you save a file, from a website for example, the file will be saved automatically to your tablet. You can find these files in the *My Files* app. You can see how this works by saving the table of contents (PDF file) from this book:

☞ **Open the *Internet* app** 🐾**31**

☞ **Open the www.visualsteps.com/samsungandroid5 web page** 🐾**32**

You will see the website that goes with this book. This is how you download the table of contents:

☞ **If necessary, zoom in on the website** 🐾**33**

👉 **Tap**
Table of contents

A part of the window may now be enlarged:

👉 **Tap**
Table of contents

Now the download process will begin. This is indicated by the 📥 icon at the top left-hand side of your screen.

You can find the file in the *Notification Panel*.

 Go back to the home screen 3

 Open the *Notification Panel* 1

Here you can see the downloaded files. To open the file:

 **Tap**

781.pdf

Download complete.

You will see a window with the apps you can use to open a PDF file.

Drive PDF Viewer

 **Tap**

 **Tap JUST ONCE**

The file will be opened:

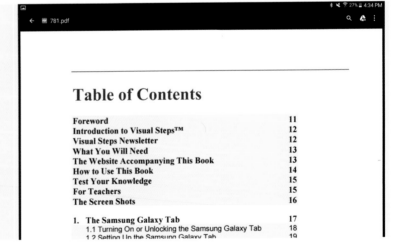

You can also find other files using the *My Files* app, for instance, downloaded files such as photos and videos that have been saved to your tablet. You can search for the file you just downloaded with this app.

☞ **Go back to the home screen** 🐾³

☞ **Tap** ▦, My Files

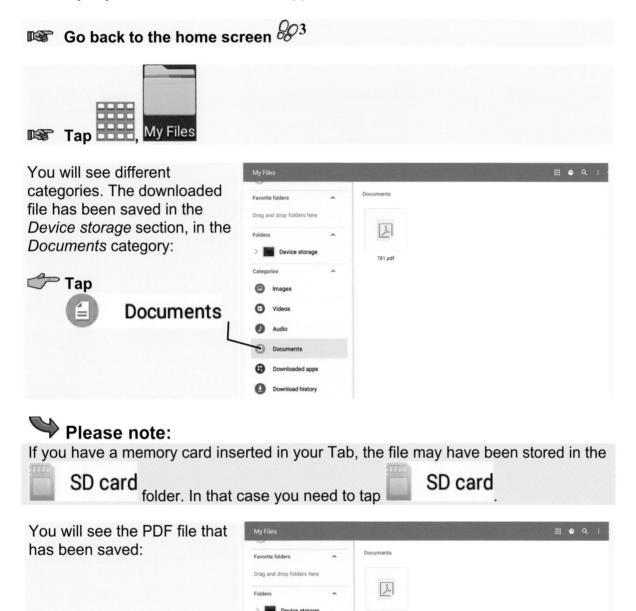

You will see different categories. The downloaded file has been saved in the *Device storage* section, in the *Documents* category:

☞ **Tap** 📄 **Documents**

👉 **Please note:**

If you have a memory card inserted in your Tab, the file may have been stored in the ▦ **SD card** folder. In that case you need to tap ▦ **SD card**.

You will see the PDF file that has been saved:

If you tap a file name, the file will be opened. For now this will not be necessary.

You can use this same method to find all sorts of files on your Tab. For example, any pictures you take in the exercises for *Chapter 7 Photos and Video* can be found in the *Images* folder. You can read more about transferring photos to your Tab from a memory card in the *Tip Transfer photos from a memory card to the Tab* at the end of *Chapter 7 Photos and Video*.

If you want to delete the downloaded file:

☞ **Tap and hold down**

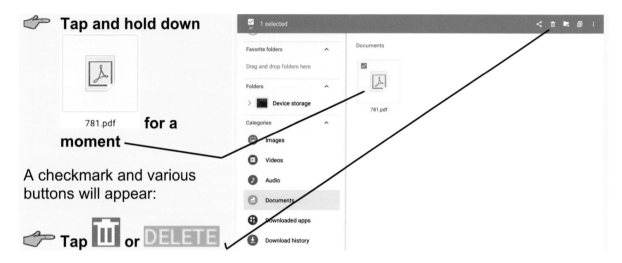

781.pdf **for a moment**

A checkmark and various buttons will appear:

☞ **Tap 🗑 or DELETE**

You will need to confirm this action:

☞ **Tap OK or DELETE**

Delete

1 item will be deleted.

CANCEL OK

You can return to the home screen of the app like this:

☞ **Press the Back key** ⤺

☞ **Go back to the home screen** 👣³

5.6 Closing Apps

By now you have used various apps on your Samsung Galaxy Tab. After you have worked with an app, you have always gone back to the home screen. When you do this, some of the apps are not actually closed and will stay active in the background. This is usually not a problem, because the Samsung Galaxy Tab uses hardly any energy (or no energy at all) when it is locked. It also makes the app accessible right away, when you unlock the tablet. But if you really want to close or quit a particular app, you can do that as follows:

☞ **Press the Recent Apps key**

You will see the apps you have recently used:

☞ **Tap the ✕ in the top right-hand corner of an app, for example**

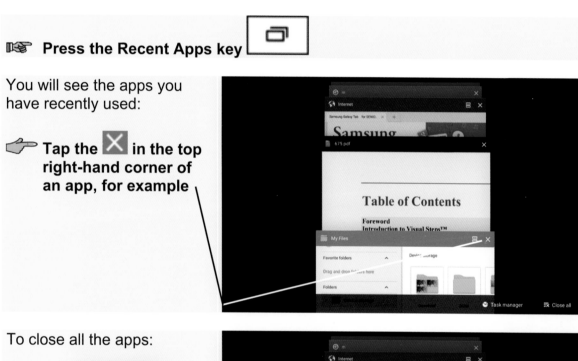

To close all the apps:

☞ **Tap** Close all

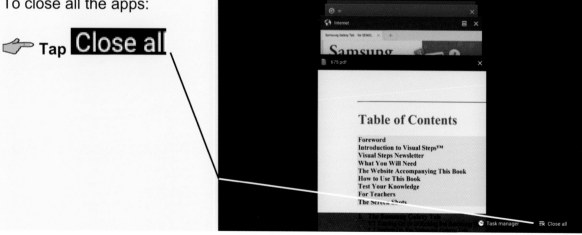

☞ **Lock or turn off the Samsung Galaxy Tab, if you wish** ⚘⁸

In this chapter you have learned how to use the *Maps* and *My Files* apps, among other things, and you have learned how to find items on your Tab. In the *Tips* at the end of this chapter you will find a summary and brief description of the apps that have not been discussed at length in this book.

5.7 Background Information

Dictionary

Download history	This folder in the *My Files* app provides contains the files that have been downloaded to the tablet.
Maps	An app with which you can find addresses and locations, get directions, and view satellite photos.
My Files	This app gives you access to the files stored on your Tab.
Search	Also called *Google Search*. The search function on the Samsung Galaxy Tab.
Street View	A service by *Google* that offers panoramic views on street level.

Source: User manual Samsung Galaxy Tab, Wikipedia

5.8 Tips

 Tip

Extensive information in Maps

You can find other information about many locations, such as the address or website link:

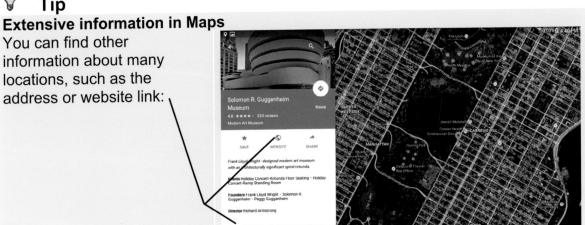

The various buttons in this screen can perform the following actions:

Use this button to save the location as a bookmark.

Use this button to share information about the location with others.

Use this button to get directions.

 Drag the pane upwards

You may also see reviews posted by previous visitors:

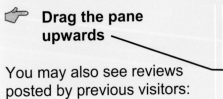

Tip

Traffic information
In the *Maps* app you can display a layer with traffic information:

 Tap ⬛ and check the box ✅ by All traffic

The speed of the traffic is indicated by a color:

Green: the traffic speed is normal.

Yellow/orange: the traffic speed has slowed down.

Red: indicates very slow traffic.

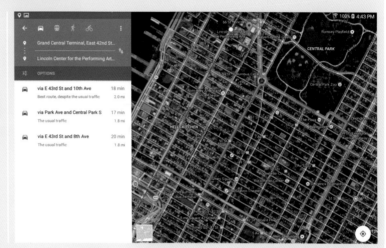

⬛ indicates an incident on the road and ⬛ is shown when a road is closed.
⬛ shows a construction zone.

 Tip

Settings for the Google Search app
You can determine which apps the *Google Search* app can search through:

 **Tap**

In the *Google Search* app:

Tap G in the address bar

In the top left-hand corner of the screen:

 **Tap ☰**

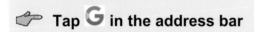

- Continue on the next page -

☞ Tap **Settings**

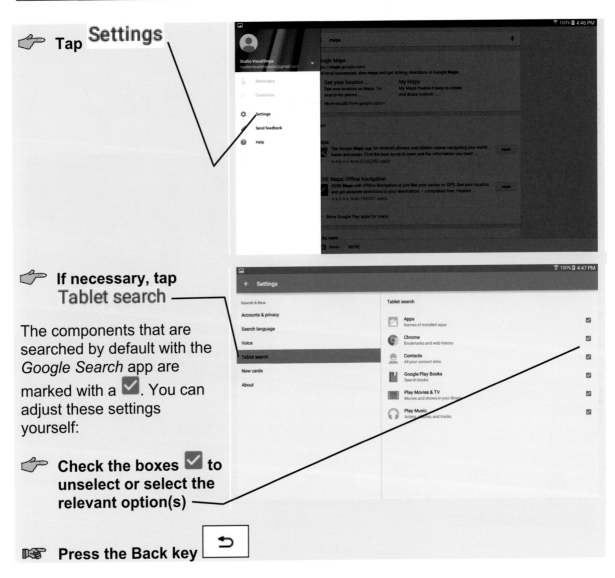

☞ **If necessary, tap**
Tablet search

The components that are
searched by default with the
Google Search app are
marked with a ☑. You can
adjust these settings
yourself:

☞ **Check the boxes ☑ to**
unselect or select the
relevant option(s)

☞ **Press the Back key** ⬅

💡 **Tip**

Summary of other apps
Your Samsung Galaxy Tab has many other standard apps installed that are not
discussed in this book. Below you can find a brief description of these apps. The
apps that are discussed in the next chapters are not listed on the next page.

Please note: not all apps are available on all tablets. It is possible that you need to

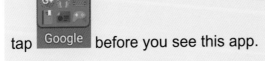

tap **Google** before you see this app.

- Continue on the next page -

Alarm

You can use this app to set an alarm for any time you want.

On some tablets this option is available in the Clock app.
Calculator.

Calculator

Chrome

Google's Internet browser.

Drive

Google Drive is an app that allows you to create, edit, and share documents. The documents that are created, edited, or uploaded with this app can be synchronized with a computer that has *Google Drive* installed.

Dropbox

You can use the *Dropbox* app to save and share photos and documents. For example, you can take a picture with your Tab, save it, and open it directly on your computer, provided you have installed *Dropbox* there as well.

Google+

A social network site by *Google*. You need to use your *Google* account for this service, and create a profile.

Google
Settings

You can use this app to adjust the settings of some functions provided by *Google*.

Hancom
Office Viewer

An Office suite that includes *Hword* (text editor), *Hcell* (spreadsheet), and *Hshow* (presentation software). With this suite you can open and edit *Microsoft Office* files, and view PDF files.

- Continue on the next page -

You can use this app to make video calls on your Samsung Galaxy Tab. In order to use *Hangouts* you need to have an Internet connection and a *Google* account. Your contacts will also need to have a *Google* account and use *Hangouts*.

This app provides help information regarding the use of the device and the apps, or the configuration of important settings.

On the Samsung Galaxy Tabs with Wi-Fi and 3G/4G you can find the *Messaging* app. You can use this app to an send and receive text messages. Your mobile service provider will charge you for this service.

You can use this app to make phone calls. Only for Tabs with Wi-Fi + 3G/4G.

An app that provides access to *Google Photos*.

Use this app to read books on your Tab.

This app can be used to download free and paid games. You will need to have a *Samsung* account in order to use this service.

- Continue on the next page -

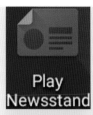

Play Newsstand

Play Newsstand gives you additional options for viewing the news items that interest you the most. You can also view news and background articles that contain audio and video.

Play Movies & TV

You can use this app to download, rent, and watch movies and TV series.

Play Music

An app that provides access to your *Google Play* music library, on every computer and on up to ten *Android* devices. All your music will be saved online, so you do not need to worry about synchronizing or storage space.

S Voice

This app lets you give voice commands to your Tab, for example, to make a call to a certain phone number, send messages, take notes, or execute other tasks.

Galaxy Apps

Galaxy Apps is an online store owned by Samsung, where you can download both free and paid apps. In order to do this you will need to have a Samsung account.

Samsung GO

An app that keeps you posted on the latest news and current information.

SideSync

You can use this app to operate the screen of your smartphone from your tablet.

Video

An app with which you can rent movies, at a certain rate.

- Continue on the next page -

You can use this app to open *Google*, and give voice commands.

 An app that lets you watch videos on *YouTube*.

 Tip
Play Books
You can use the *Play Books* app to download and read books on your Tab:

☞ **Open the *Play Books* app**

You will see a start screen with a various categories. For now, you can skip this:

☞ **Tap**

You can get samples of new books, if you wish. For now, this will not be necessary:

☞ **If necessary, tap NO THANKS**

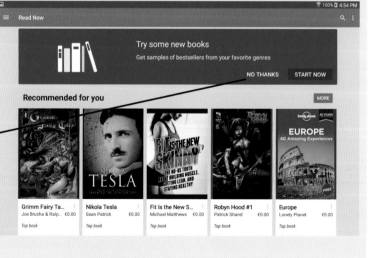

- Continue on the next page -

You can search various categories.

You can look for a book by using the search function:

☞ **Tap**

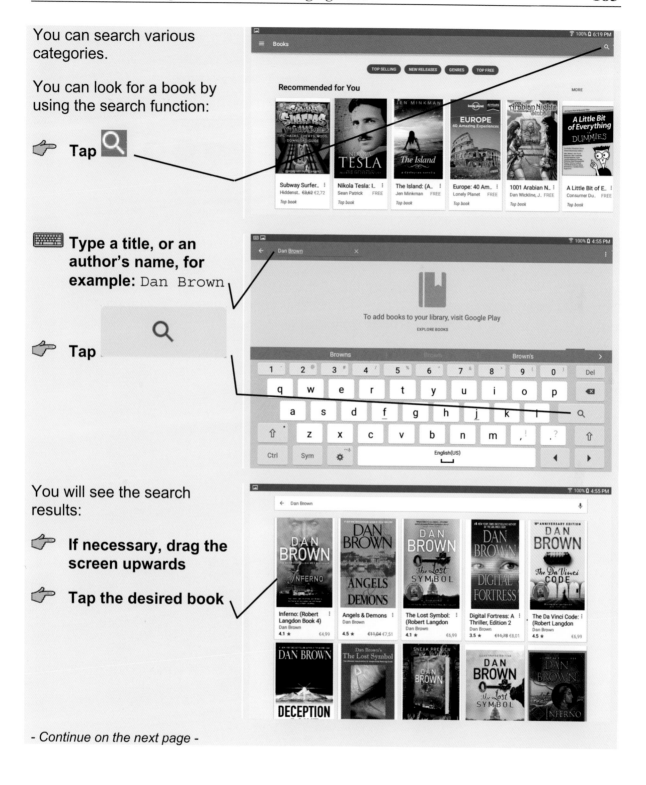

⌨ **Type a title, or an author's name, for example:** `Dan Brown`

☞ **Tap**

You will see the search results:

☞ **If necessary, drag the screen upwards**

☞ **Tap the desired book**

- Continue on the next page -

If you would like to sample a few pages, tap

FREE SAMPLE :

If you want to purchase the

book, tap   BUY   4,99 :

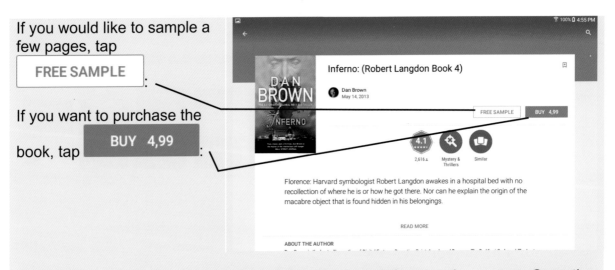

When you have made your selection, follow the instructions on the screen. Once the book has been downloaded, it will appear directly on your screen. By tapping the right-hand side of the screen you can go to the next page.

6. Downloading Apps

In the previous chapters you have become acquainted with a number of the standard apps that are pre-installed on the Samsung Galaxy Tab. But there are many more things you can do with this handy tablet. In the *Play Store* you will find thousands of additional apps that can be purchased or acquired for free.

There are far too many apps to list all of them in this book. There are apps for newspapers and magazines, weather forecasts, games, recipes, and sports results. You will undoubtedly find an app that interests you!

In this chapter you will learn how to download a free app from the *Play Store*. If you want to purchase an app, you can use a *Google Gift Card* to pay for it, link a credit card to your *Google* account or pay through you PayPal account. It only takes a few steps to do this.

Once you have purchased some apps, you can change the order in which they are arranged on the screen of your Tab. You can even create folders for your apps and store related apps in them. You can also delete the apps you no longer want to use.

In this chapter you will learn how to:

- download and install a free app;
- redeem a *Google Gift Card*;
- purchase and install an app;
- move apps;
- save apps in a folder;
- delete apps.

 Please note:

In order to buy and download apps in the *Play Store*, you need to have connected a *Google* account to your tablet. If you do not yet have a *Google* account, you can read how to create one in *section 1.12 Creating and Adding a Google Account*.

 Please note:

While you are using your Tab, you may see some screens that provide additional information about the operation of an app or the keyboard. You can read the information and tap **DONE** or **OK** afterwards.

6.1 Downloading a Free App

In the *Play Store* you will find thousands of free apps. This how you open the *Play Store*:

☞ **Turn on** 👣^{4} **or unlock the Samsung Galaxy Tab** 👣^{9}

You may see a welcome screen first, with some information. If necessary, tap **GET STARTED**.

The *Play Store* is opened:

You will see the **APPS & GAMES** page, where a number of popular apps are highlighted. To see more apps:

☞ **Drag the screen across the apps with your finger from right to left**

You can also view a list of categories with all the available apps:

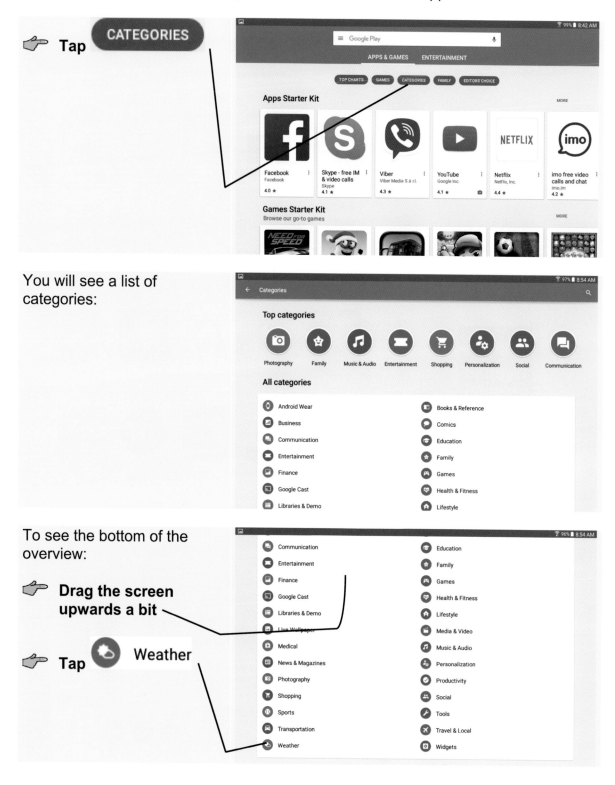

☞ **Tap** CATEGORIES

You will see a list of categories:

To see the bottom of the overview:

☞ **Drag the screen upwards a bit**

☞ **Tap** ☁ **Weather**

You will see a long list of popular apps that can be purchased. To view the most popular free apps in this same category:

☞ **If necessary, tap**
TOP APPS

You will see all sorts of free apps regarding the weather. Take a look at a popular free app:

☞ **If necessary, drag the screen upwards**

☞ **Tap**

A screen will be opened with additional information about this app. If you want to download the app:

☞ **Tap** INSTALL

You will see a list of permissions required, in order for the app to function properly on your tablet. You will need to accept these permissions:

The app will be installed. After the app has been installed, you can open it:

You may see an advertisement:

Tap ⊠

If necessary, tap the screen

You will see the *The Weather Channel* app. This app will keep you posted on the current weather conditions:

Go back to the home screen ✂³

Tip

Update apps

In the *Tips* at the end of this chapter you can read how to update an app. From time to time, an update may be offered containing bug fixes or additional functionality.

 Tip

Managing apps

The new app will be placed on the first free spot in the apps list. If the page is full, a new page will be created. In *section 6.3 Managing apps* you can read how to move apps around on a page and between pages.

In the next section you will learn how to purchase an app.

6.2 Downloading a Purchased App

If you want to acquire an app that must be purchased first, you can pay for it with *Google Gift Card* credit, a debit or a credit card, or a PayPal account. When you try to download an app that is not free, you will be asked which one of these payment methods you want to use.

 HELP! I do not have a Google Gift Card, credit card, or a PayPal account.

You can purchase a *Google Gift Card* and redeem it in the *Play Store*. You can read more about gift cards on http://play.google.com/intl/en-US_us/about/giftcards/.
The *Play Store* also accepts payment by credit card. If you do not have a credit card, you could consider getting a prepaid Visa card, MasterCard, or American Express credit card. When you have done this, you can 'charge' this card with any amount you wish. With a prepaid credit card you can purchase any item as long as it does not exceed the pre-deposited amount on the credit card. Because of this, the risk of making online payments is quite small.
Another payment method is called PayPal. PayPal acts as an intermediary, so your bank account information will not be disclosed when you pay for an item in the *Play Store*. You can pay through PayPal and choose whether to pay with your regular bank account, a debit or a credit card, or with your PayPal credit. More information can be found on the PayPal website: www.paypal.com.

 Please note:

In this example a *Google Gift Card* is used. If you do not have such a card, you can use a debit card, a credit card, or your PayPal account. You can also just read through this section, or if available, you can install the free version of this app.

☞ **Open the *Play Store*** 🐾¹⁹

You will see the page for *The Weather Channel* app again. This is how you go back to the *Play Store*:

👉 **Tap** ⬅️

Previously, you have searched for an app by using the categories. But you can also search directly for the name of the app you want to download:

👉 **If necessary, scroll upwards a bit**

👉 **Tap** 🔍

In this example, we are looking for the name of a popular game. In this game, the goal is to help Swampy the alligator guide water to his broken shower:

⌨️ **Type:** my water

👉 **Tap** 🔍

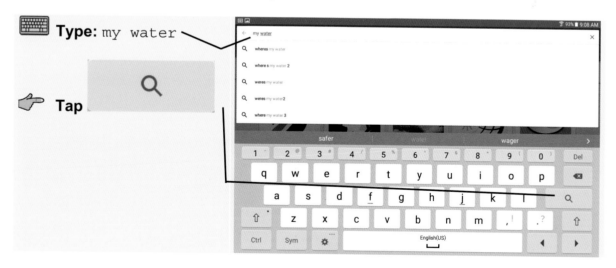

This app comes in both a free and a paid version ($1.99). For this exercise, we are selecting the paid version. If necessary, scroll downwards a bit:

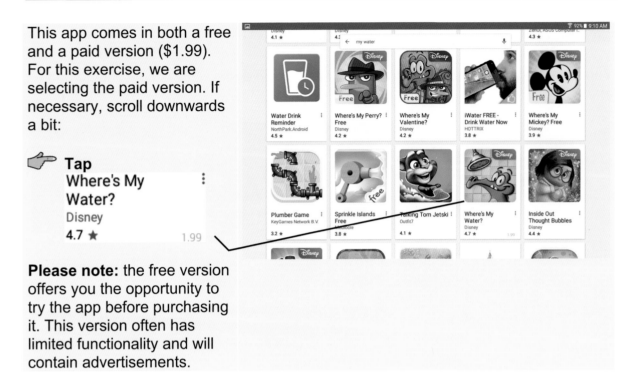

 Tap
Where's My Water?
Disney
4.7 ★   1.99

Please note: the free version offers you the opportunity to try the app before purchasing it. This version often has limited functionality and will contain advertisements.

 Please note:

In the next few steps an app will be purchased. You can decide for yourself whether you want to follow the steps to buy this app. Of course, you do not need to buy the same app as shown in this example.

 Please note:

You can only do the following steps if you have a *Google Gift Card*. If you do not have a *Google Gift Card*, you can just read through the rest of this section, or use another payment method such as a debit card, credit card, or PayPal account.

In this example, the app that is purchased costs $1.99:

Tap 1.99

You will see the window again where the required permissions for this app are displayed:

☞ **Tap** ACCEPT

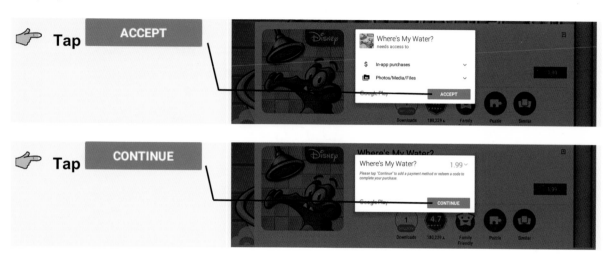

☞ **Tap** CONTINUE

You are going to redeem the credit on your *Google Gift Card*:

☞ **Tap** ▶ Redeem

Please note: if you are using a debit or a credit card, you tap 💳 **Add credit or debit card** and follow the instructions. If you want to pay with PayPal, you tap 🅿 **Add PayPal** and follow the instructions.

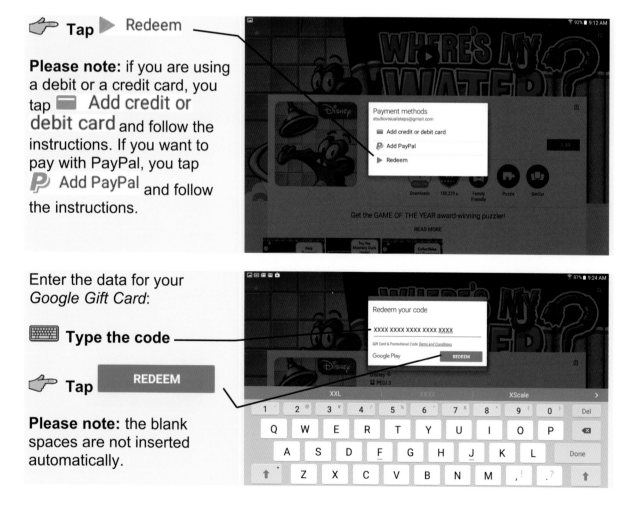

Enter the data for your *Google Gift Card*:

⌨ **Type the code**

☞ **Tap** REDEEM

Please note: the blank spaces are not inserted automatically.

The credit has been added to your *Google Play* credit. You can proceed:

☞ **Tap** 1.99

 Please note:

If your *Google Gift Card* has already been activated, you may see fewer windows, or the windows may be displayed in a different order and not match the order described in this section. In that case, just follow the instructions in the windows that you see.

☞ **Tap** BUY

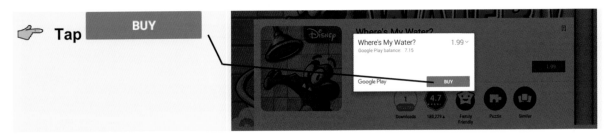

As an extra security measure, you will be asked to enter the password for your *Google* account:

⌨ **Type the password for your *Google* account**

☞ **Tap** CONFIRM

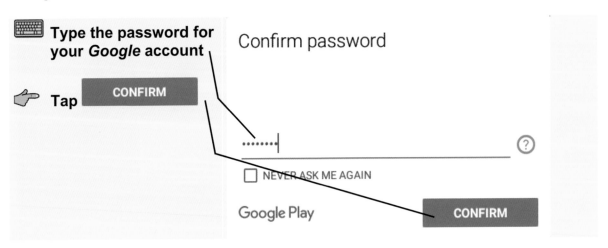

Confirm password

⬤⬤⬤⬤⬤⬤⬤|

☐ NEVER ASK ME AGAIN

Google Play   CONFIRM

Please note:

It is safer not to check the NEVER ASK ME AGAIN option. If you select this option, purchases can be made in the *Play Store* and charged to your *Google Gift Card*, debit card, credit card, or PayPal account, without having to enter a password. In some games you can buy fake money in the app (while you are playing the game), and use it to bargain with. This fake money is paid for with your credit on your *Google Gift Card*, debit card, credit card, or PayPal account. If you let your children or grandchildren play such a game, for example, they will be able to purchase items without you noticing it. So it is much safer to enter the password every time you want to buy something.

You will briefly see a window with a message about the payment being successful:

You can choose how often you would like to confirm your password:

 Tap the desired option

Payment successful

You can choose to be prompted for a password once every 30 minutes for purchases of all forms of digital content, including in-app purchases. However, authentication is always required for purchases through Google Play within apps designated for ages 12 and under.

How often would you like to confirm your password for purchases?

EVERY TIME   **EVERY 30 MIN**

You may see a window with information about the app again:

 If necessary, tap   INSTALL

The app is downloaded and installed:

Where's My Water?
Disney
PEGI 3

5.16MB/69.47MB   7% ✕

In a short while, the app will be installed. This is indicated by the   **OPEN**   button that is now displayed.

You can view the app you just downloaded a little later on. First, we will go back to the store:

Go back to the start screen of the *Play Store*:

☞ **Tap ←**

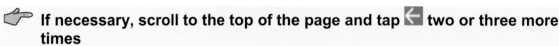

☞ **If necessary, scroll to the top of the page and tap ← two or three more times**

☞ **Go back to the home screen of the Samsung Galaxy Tab** 🐾**3**

6.3 Managing Apps

You can arrange the apps on your screen in any order you wish. You do this by moving them:

For example, you will see the newly downloaded apps on the home screen:

↘ **Please note:**

In order to carry out the next few steps, you need to have installed at least two apps. If you have not purchased an app, you can download another free app that interests you, as described in *section 6.1 Downloading a Free App*. Or you can use other apps to perform the steps in this section.

You can arrange the apps any way you want. This is how you move an app:

👉 **Place your finger on**

🩹 HELP! I do not see The Weather Channel app on this spot.

On your tablet, *The Weather Channel* app may not be present on this screen. In that case you can use another app to work with in this section, or leaf forward to the screen that actually contains this app.

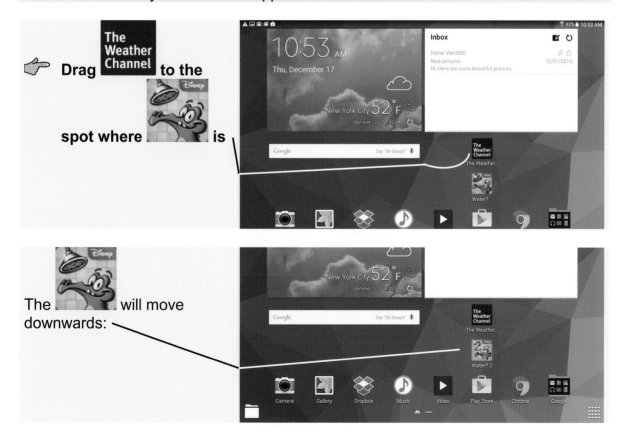

👉 **Drag** [The Weather Channel] **to the**

spot where [ ] **is**

The [ ] **will move downwards:**

You can also move an app to another page. This is how you place an app on the second page:

☞ **Place your finger on**

The Weather Channel

☞ **Drag** The Weather Channel **to the right-hand border of the screen**

When you see another page:

☞ **Release** The Weather Channel

Now the app has moved to the other page:

You can also store apps together in a folder. First, move the app back to the first page:

☞ **Place** *The Weather Channel* **app on the first page** ✂28

👉 **Place your finger on** **The Weather Channel**

👉 **Drag** **The Weather Channel** **to** 📁 **Create folder**

If you do not see 📁 **Create folder**, you can create a folder by dragging the apps on top of each other:

👉 **Drag** **The Weather Channel** **on top of**

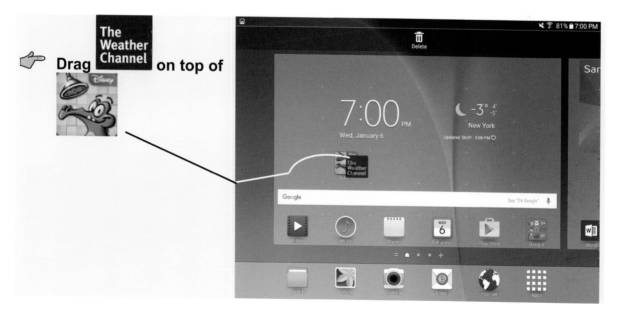

You will see the *Create folder* window. In this example you will not be entering a name for the folder:

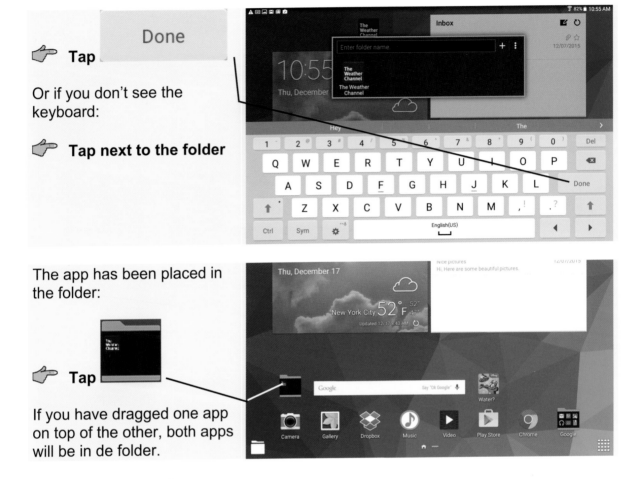

Tap Done

Or if you don't see the keyboard:

Tap next to the folder

The app has been placed in the folder:

Tap

If you have dragged one app on top of the other, both apps will be in de folder.

The folder is opened:

If you wish, you can enter a name for the folder, by Unnamed folder:

For now this will not be necessary.

Tap next to the folder

If necessary, you can add the other app you have downloaded to the new folder:

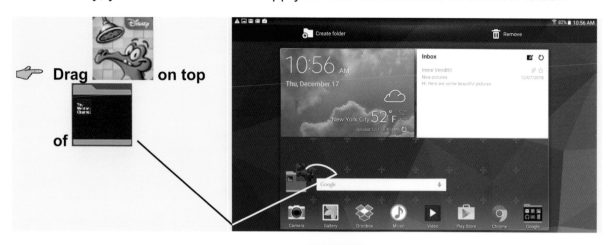

☞ **Drag** [Disney app] **on top**

of [The Weather Channel folder]

Now both apps have been included in the  folder. This is how you view the content of the folder:

☞ **Tap** [The Weather Channel folder]

You will see both apps in the folder:

If you want, you can add some more apps to this folder.

This is how you remove an app from the folder again:

👉 **Drag the app away from the folder**

Now the app is on its own again, on the home screen:

You can also delete the folder. The apps that are stored in the folder will not be deleted:

👉 **Drag the folder to**
🗑 **Remove**

When you see 🗑 **Remove** :

👉 **Release the folder**

It is possible that *The Weather Channel* app is no longer located on the home

screen. You can find it by tapping the button. This will open the list showing all the apps. If there is a second page with apps, you can open it by dragging the screen from right to left.

6.4 Deleting an App

If you are unhappy with an app you have downloaded, you can delete it. You do this using the *Play Store*.

☞ **Tap** Play Store

☞ **Tap** ▤

☞ **Tap** My apps & games

You will see the apps list. You can delete the apps you have downloaded from the *Play Store*. In this example we will delete the app called *The Weather Channel*:

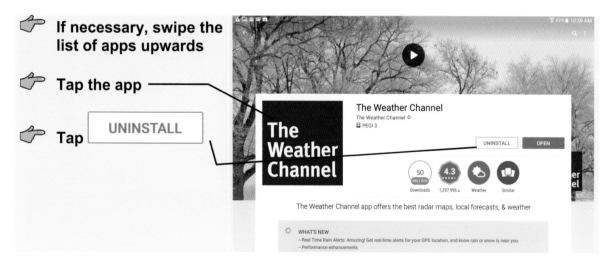

☞ **If necessary, swipe the list of apps upwards**

☞ **Tap the app**

☞ **Tap** UNINSTALL

If you really want to uninstall this app:

The app will be removed from the list.

In this chapter you have learned how to acquire new apps by using the *Play Store*.

6.5 Background Information

Dictionary

App Short for *application*, a program for the Samsung Galaxy Tab.

Google account A combination of an email address and a password. You need to have a *Google* account in order to download apps from the *Play Store*.

Google Gift Card A prepaid card with which you can purchase items from the *Play Store*.

PayPal PayPal is a service that acts as an intermediary, so your bank account information is not displayed when you pay for something in the *Play Store*. When you pay through PayPal, you can choose whether you want to use your bank account, your debit or credit card, or your PayPal credit.

Play Store An online store where you can download free and paid apps.

Update Install the most recent version of the Tab's operating system, or of particular apps.

Source: User manual Samsung Galaxy Tab

6.6 Tips

 Tip

Update apps
After a while, the apps that are installed on your Tab will be updated for free. These updates may be necessary to solve certain problems (often called bug fixes). An update can also contain new functions or additional options, such as a new level in a game app. You can check for updates yourself:

☞ **Open the *Play Store*** 🦶[19]

 **Tap**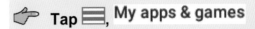

In this example, there are updates available for multiple apps:

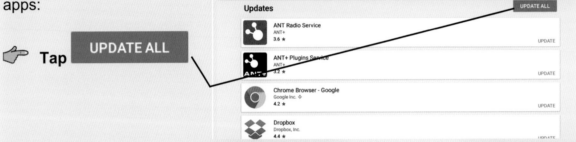

☞ **Tap**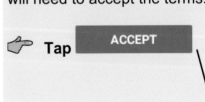

You may see various screens. For example, you will need to accept the terms:

☞ **Tap** ACCEPT

- Continue on the next page -

The update(s) will be downloaded and installed. This may take a few minutes. The apps are updated. Some apps will be updated automatically, as soon as a new update becomes available. If you want to change this setting:

☞ **Tap the app**

At the top right-hand side of the screen:

☞ **Tap** ⦙

Uncheck the ☑ box by **Auto-update**.

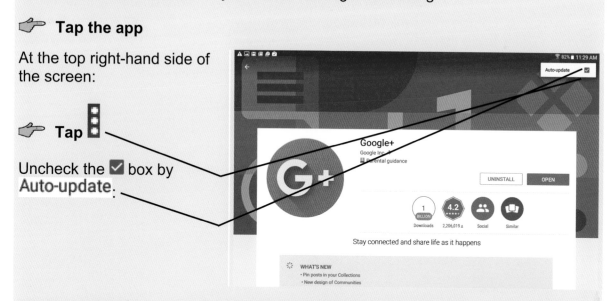

Please note: if you are using a mobile Internet connection through 3G/4G, these automatic updates may cost you money. It is better to change these settings, so that apps are updated only when a Wi-Fi Internet connection is available.

☞ **Tap** ☰

☞ **If necessary, scroll down a bit**

☞ **Tap** ⚙ **Settings**

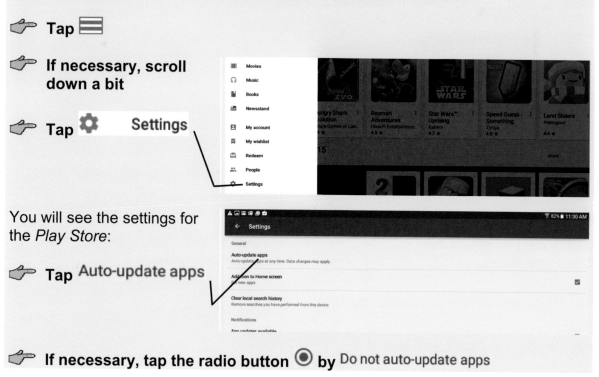

You will see the settings for the *Play Store*:

☞ **Tap** Auto-update apps

☞ **If necessary, tap the radio button** ◉ **by** Do not auto-update apps

Tip

Download a purchased app for the second time
If you have uninstalled a purchased app, you can always download and re-install it later on, free of charge. You will need to use the same *Google* account as you did before, in order to do this.

☞ **Open the *Play Store*** 🦶¹⁹

👆 **Tap** ▤, **My apps & games**

👆 **Tap** ALL

👆 **If necessary, swipe the apps list upwards**

Where's My Water?
Disney ✦
4.7 ★

👆 **Tap**

The *Play Store* remembers that you have previously purchased the app. Instead of 1.99 you will see the **INSTALL** button.

👆 **Tap** INSTALL

In the next window:

👆 **Tap** ACCEPT

The app will be downloaded and installed. You will not be charged for this download.

 Tip

Using the Facebook app
If you use *Facebook*, you can download the *Facebook* app and use it on your Tab.

☞ **Download the *Facebook* app** 🦶²³

☞ **Open the *Facebook* app** 🦶²⁵

- Continue on the next page -

You will need to sign in with your *Facebook* account, one-time only:

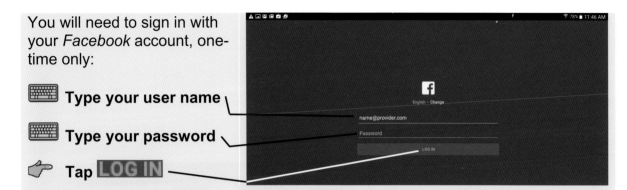

⌨ **Type your user name**

⌨ **Type your password**

☞ **Tap** LOG IN

On your News Feed page, you will see your friends' messages, and those of the celebrities or companies you follow. The messages you post on your own page, will appear in your friends' News Feed.

You can tap ✏ STATUS to post a status update on your own *Facebook* page. You can tap 📷 PHOTO to select or take a photo, and post it on your page, with or without a caption. You can tap 📍 CHECK IN to post a message with your current location on your page.

If you want to *like* a message:

☞ **By the message, tap** 👍 Like

If you want to comment on a message:

☞ **By the message, tap** 💬 Comment

⌨ **Type your message**

☞ **Tap** ➤ **to post the message**

Or, if you want to share a message:

☞ **By the message, tap** ↪ Share

If someone reacts to your post, or comments on a message to which you have commented as well, the 🌐 button will turn into 🌐. In the same way you will see new friend requests by 👥, and new private messages by 🗔.

- Continue on the next page -

If you would like to view your own timeline:

☞ **Tap** ▬

☞ **Tap your name**

You will see the messages on your timeline.

You can use the search box to find friends or pages:

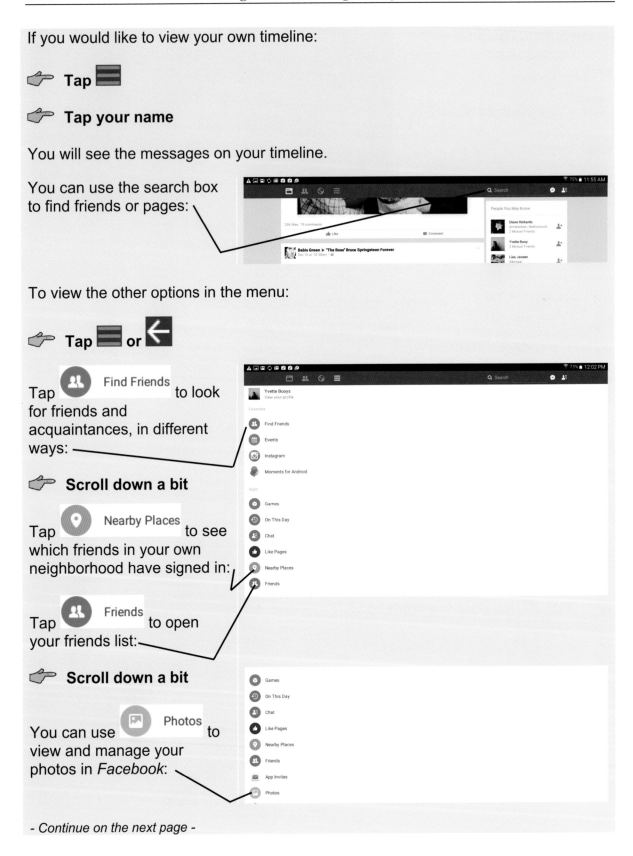

To view the other options in the menu:

☞ **Tap** ▬ **or** ⬅

Tap **Find Friends** to look for friends and acquaintances, in different ways:

☞ **Scroll down a bit**

Tap **Nearby Places** to see which friends in your own neighborhood have signed in:

Tap **Friends** to open your friends list:

☞ **Scroll down a bit**

You can use **Photos** to view and manage your photos in *Facebook*:

- Continue on the next page -

At the bottom you will find the buttons for the help options and for changing the settings. If you stay signed in, new data will be retrieved as soon as you open the *Facebook* app. If you prefer to sign off, you can do so like this:

👉 **Tap** , LOG OUT

💡 **Tip**

Using the Twitter app

If you use *Twitter*, you can download the *Twitter* app and use it on your tablet.

👉 **Download the *Twitter* app** 👣²³

👉 **Open the *Twitter* app** 👣²⁵

You will need to sign in with your *Twitter* account, one-time only:

👉 **Tap**

⌨ **Type your user name**

👉 **Tap** Next

⌨ **Type your password**

👉 **Tap** Log in

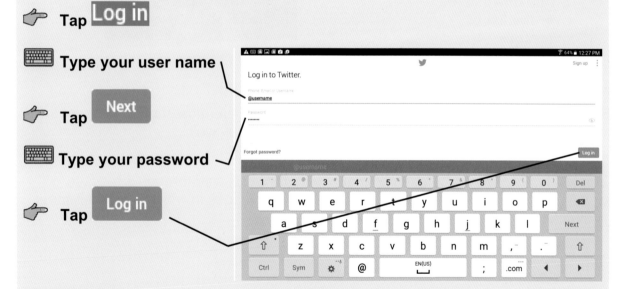

You may see a screen regarding SNS permission, in order to use your account: You may see a screen regarding permission for Samsung Galaxy to use your account:

👉 **Tap**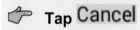

- Continue on the next page -

Twitter wants to use your current location:

 If necessary, tap OK

Twitter would like to use your current location to customize your experience.

DON'T ALLOW ———— OK

You will see your timeline, with the latest tweets of the people or companies you follow. Your own tweets will appear in the timeline of your followers.

This is how you load new tweets:

 Swipe downwards over the list of messages

Use the buttons in the menu to do the following:

Tap ![twitter icon] to open the *Twitter* home page. Here you see the most recent tweets of the people or companies you follow, and your own tweets as well.

Tap ![notifications icon] to open a list of all the comments you have received through a tweet to which you have replied. You will also see all the messages in which your user name is mentioned.

Tap ![envelope icon] to send a private message to someone you follow.

- Continue on the next page -

Tap 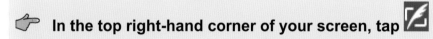 to look for other *Twitter* users.

Tap Q and Q Search Twitter to look for tweets, by their subject or name. You will also see list of popular tweets and trends.

Tap ⋮, Visual Steps (your name) to go to the page that contains your profile information. This page also contains links to the timeline with the tweets you have sent, the accounts you follow, and your own followers. This page is visible to everyone. Here you can also access your private messages. These are only visible to yourself.

This is how you send a new tweet:

☞ **In the top right-hand corner of your screen, tap** ✎

⌨ **Type your message**

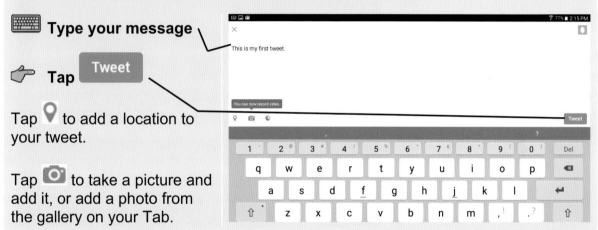

☞ **Tap** Tweet

Tap ♀ to add a location to your tweet.

Tap 📷 to take a picture and add it, or add a photo from the gallery on your Tab.

Your tweet will appear at the top of your timeline. Your followers will see your tweet appear in their timeline.

💡 **Tip**

Antivirus app
Just like on your computer, viruses can infect your Tab too. Nowadays, an antivirus app is a necessity. Although there are various antivirus apps available, most of their options are very similar. In this *Tip* the *Tablet AntiVirus Security Free* app by AVG Mobile is downloaded.

☞ **Download the *Tablet AntiVirus Security Free* app by AVG Mobile** 23

- Continue on the next page -

Please note: make sure to select the version suited for a tablet. You can recognize this version by the word .

Activate the app:

 Tap OPEN

On the *Tablet AntiVirus Security Free* app:

 Tap GET STARTED, NO THANKS

You will see the app's start screen:

For now you do not need to change the settings, but you can allow the app to start scanning your tablet right away. To do that:

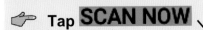 Tap SCAN NOW

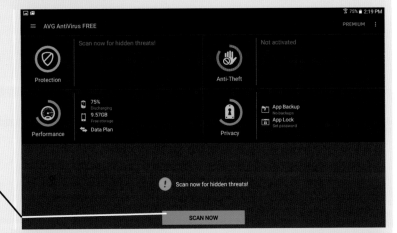

During the scanning process you will see:

After the Tab has been scanned, you will see a screen with various options. To view the scan results:

☞ Tap
← Scan Results

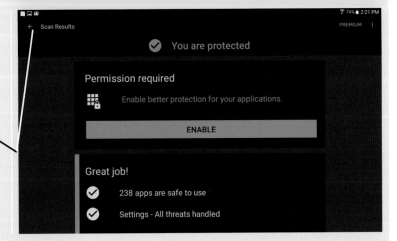

- Continue on the next page -

If no viruses have been found, you can set the time interval at which the Tab will automatically scan your tablet. On the home screen:

☞ **Tap**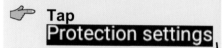

On the next screen:

☞ **Tap**

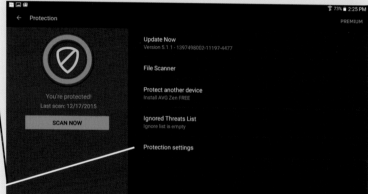

On the next screen:

☞ **Tap**
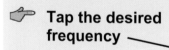

You will see a screen where you can select the frequency:

☞ **Tap the desired frequency**

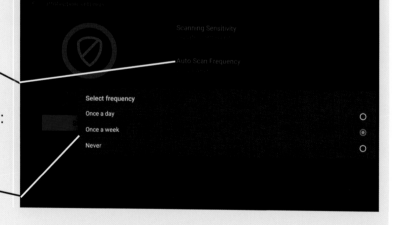

- Continue on the next page -

Other options in the *Protections settings* segment are:

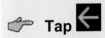 **Safe Web Surfing**   If you disable this function, you will not be protected while you are surfing the Internet. This is not recommended for regular usage.

Scanning Sensitivity   Here you can set the scan sensitivity.

At the top left-hand side of the screen:

☞ **Tap** ⬅

Other security options for your tablet are:

Update Now   With this option you can manually search for an update for the app.

File Scanner   Here you can indicate which folders to be scanned.

Apart from the antivirus protection, this app offers a number of additional functions:

Performance   Here you can get information about your Tab's performance. If you want more information, tap ◢ by the desired topic.

Anti-Theft   If you wish you can register your Tab for an anti-theft function. By registering, you will be able to block your Tab in case it is stolen, remotely lock the device and even find the current location of the Tab.

Privacy   Here you can secure apps with a password, or create backup copies of apps. You can temporarily try this function for fourteen days, but afterwards you will need to purchase the paid version of the app.
You can also delete data on the Tab or SD (memory) card.

Tip

Using the Skype app
Skype is a great way of communicating with friends and family. You can conduct free phone calls and video calls through the Internet. Just install the *Skype* app and create a user name, and you can search for other *Skype* users. The person you want to contact will also need to have installed the *Skype* app.

☞ **Download the free *Skype* app** ◖◗²³

☞ **Open the *Skype* app** ◖◗²⁶

⌨ **Enter your *Skype* name and password**

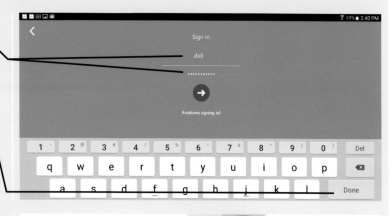

☞ **Tap**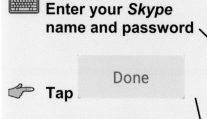

You can also create a new account, if you wish.

You will see the people who are already in your contacts list:

Use the buttons on the screen to do the following:

 Make a call.

 Send an IM (Instant Message).

 Use this button to view a menu with options for adding people or numbers.

 View a list of Settings.

- Continue on the next page -

☞ **Tap** People ⊙

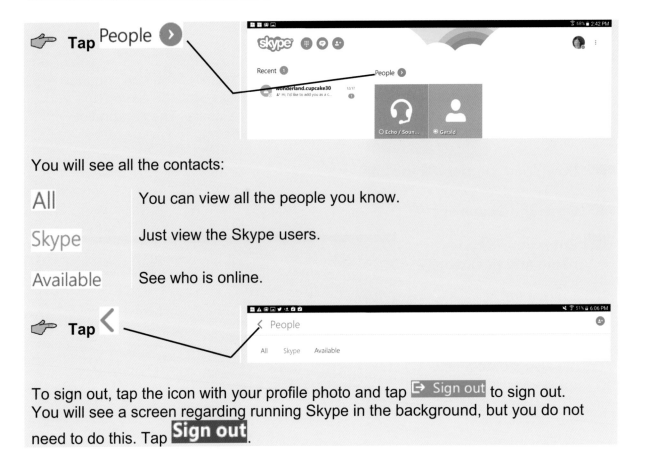

You will see all the contacts:

All	You can view all the people you know.
Skype	Just view the Skype users.
Available	See who is online.

☞ **Tap** ‹

To sign out, tap the icon with your profile photo and tap ⤷ Sign out to sign out. You will see a screen regarding running Skype in the background, but you do not need to do this. Tap **Sign out**.

7. Photos and Video

The two cameras on the Samsung Galaxy Tab offer a wealth of possibilities for taking pictures and shooting videos. You can use the *Camera* app to access both of these cameras. The camera on the back of the Tab allows you to take a picture or film an interesting object. With the front camera you can create a self-portrait.

The *Gallery* app can be used to view your photos. You can view them one at a time, or display them as a slideshow on your Tab.

To play your videos you can use the *Video* app.

In this chapter you will learn how to:

- take pictures with your Samsung Galaxy Tab;
- switch between the front and rear camera;
- film a video with your Samsung Galaxy Tab;
- view photos;
- zoom in and zoom out;
- view a slideshow;
- send a photo by email;
- print a photo;
- copy photos and videos to the computer;
- play the video you have recorded.

 Please note:

While you are using your Tab, you may see some screens that provide additional information about the operation of an app or the keyboard. You can read the information and tap DONE or OK afterwards.

7.1 Taking Pictures

You can use the *Camera* app to take pictures. This is how you open the app:

☞ **Turn on** 😕⁴ **or unlock the Samsung Galaxy Tab** 😕⁹

☞ **If necessary, tap**

☞ **Tap** Camera

You will see the image that is recorded by the camera on the back of the Tab.

☞ **Point the camera towards the object you want to photograph**

↘ **Please note:**
Make sure you have sufficient light. Some tabs are not equipped with a flash. If there is not enough light to take a picture, the picture will look grainy.

To take the picture:

☞ **Tap**

The photo will be stored on your Tab.

Tip

Zoom in and out
Spread two fingers towards or away from each other, in order to zoom in or out.

 Take two more pictures ✍**15**

 Tip

Self-portrait
You can also choose to use the camera on the front of the Samsung Galaxy Tab. This enables you to take a picture of yourself. To switch to the front camera:

 Tap

Please note: on some tabs this button is located on the right-hand side of the screen.

You will see the image of the front camera:

Now you can take a picture in the same way as you did with the rear camera.

To switch back to the rear camera:

 Tap

The other main buttons on the screen of the *Camera* app are used for the functions listed below. You may need to tap the button to view more functions. Depending on the type of tablet you have, you may see additional options or not see certain options at all.

Button	Description
	Set the photo mode. You can choose between the Auto, Beauty Face, Sound & Shot, Panorama, Sports and on some tablets Night modes. When you select a mode you will see what this mode does.
	Set a timer for an automatic recording.

Adjust the camera settings.

 Share photos. You can choose to share pictures with other devices using Wi-Fi Direct. You can share a photo with friends, or take a picture with the viewfinder of a connected device.

 Add effects to the photo.

7.2 Filming

You can also use the camera to film videos:

On some tablets you need to drag the slider before you can film videos:

☞ **If necessary, drag the slider to**

☞ **Tap**

💡 **Tip**

Sideways
If you would like to play your video on a television or a larger screen, you will need to hold your Samsung Galaxy Tab in a horizontal position (landscape mode). This will provide you with a nice full-screen image.

turns into :

On some tablets the recording will start at once. If this is not the case on your tablet, you need to start it manually:

☞ **If necessary, tap**

While you are recording the video, you will see a red circle ⬤ blinking at the top left-hand side or at the bottom of the screen.

To stop filming:

☞ **Tap**

If you want to pause the recording session and continue later on, you

tap :

On some tablets the camera will automatically revert to photo mode. If this is not happening on your tablet, you can change the *Camera* app back to photo mode again:

☞ **Drag the slider** to

☞ **Go back to the home screen** 𝄞³

7.3 Viewing Photos in the Gallery

Once you have taken a number of pictures with your Samsung Galaxy Tab, you can view them in the *Gallery* app. To open the app:

☞ **Tap** Gallery

You might see all the photos and videos you have created. You can go to the Camera album:

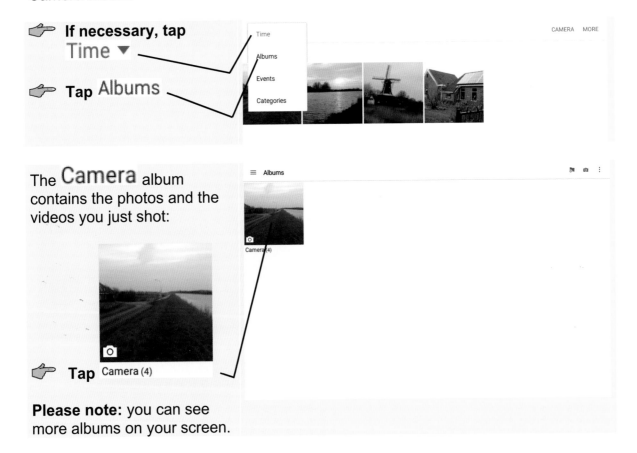

☞ **If necessary, tap**
Time ▼

☞ **Tap** Albums

The Camera album contains the photos and the videos you just shot:

☞ **Tap** Camera (4)

Please note: you can see more albums on your screen.

You will see the pictures you have taken:

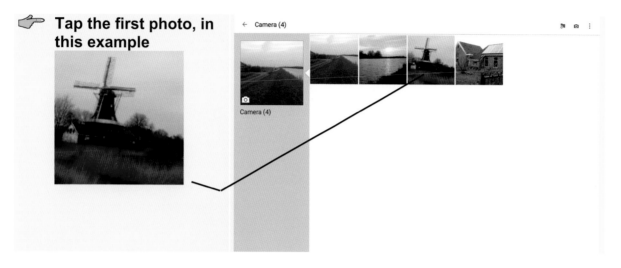

☞ **Tap the first photo, in this example**

You may see a screen regarding tags:

☞ **Tap OK**

The photo will be displayed on a full screen. This is how you leaf to the next photo:

☞ **Swipe the photo from right to left**

You will see the next photo. To go back to the previous photo:

 Swipe the photo from left to right

You can also zoom in on the photo. For this you can use the touch gestures you have previously used while surfing the Internet:

 Spread your thumb and index finger across the screen

In this way, you will zoom in on the photo:

 Tip

Move
You can also move the photo you have zoomed in on by dragging your finger across the screen.

To zoom out again:

 Move your thumb and index finger towards each other (pinch) across the

screen

You will see the regular view of the photo again.

To go back to the first photo:

 Swipe the photo from left to right

You can also view a slideshow of all the photos in an album. Here is how you do that:

 If necessary, tap the photo

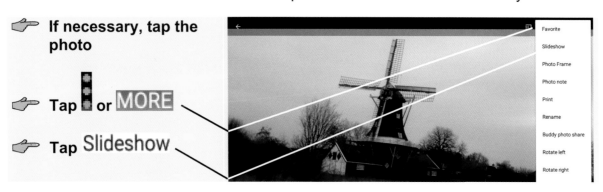

☞ **Tap** ⋮ **or** MORE

☞ **Tap** Slideshow

✕ HELP! I do not see the menu bar.
The menu bar will appear when you tap the photo.

On some tablets the slideshow starts immediately. To change settings tap the photo, tap slideshow settings.

☞ **Tap** SLIDESHOW SETTINGS

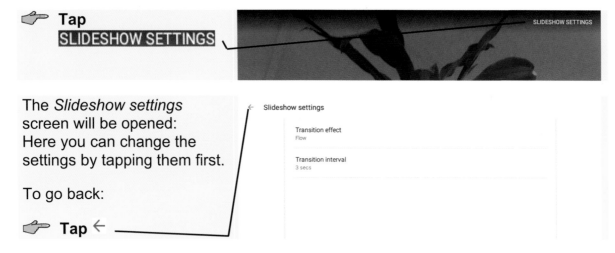

The *Slideshow settings* screen will be opened:
Here you can change the settings by tapping them first.

To go back:

☞ **Tap** ←

Slideshow settings

Transition effect
Flow

Transition interval
3 secs

If the slideshow doesn't start immediately on your tablet, you will see the effects first:

You can even add effects and music, if you wish. On the MORE tab you can select the speed and sorting method:

To start the slideshow:

☞ **Tap** START

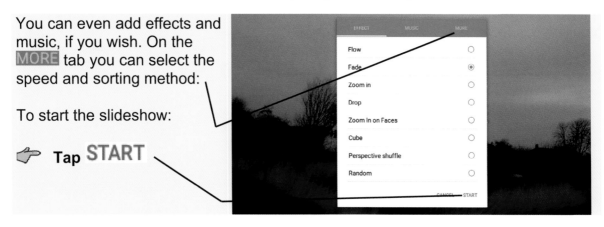

You will see the slideshow. If you have recorded a video too, this will not be displayed in the slideshow. You will only see the first frame. On some tablets you can play back the video by tapping the Play button. To stop the slideshow:

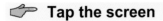 **Tap the screen**

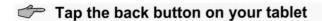 **Tap the back button on your tablet**

 **If necessary, tap** ←

You will see all of the photos again.

 Tip
Delete a photo
This is how you delete the pictures you have taken:

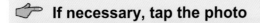 **If necessary, tap the photo**

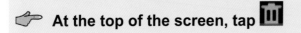 **At the top of the screen, tap** 🗑

🗑

Please note: on some tablets the icon Delete is located on the bottom of the screen.

 **Tap** OK **or** DELETE

7.4 Sending a Photo by Email

If you have made a nice photo on your Tab, you can share it with others by email. You start by opening the photo you want to send:

📖 **Open the desired photo** ∂∂20

☞ **Tap the photo**

☞ **Tap**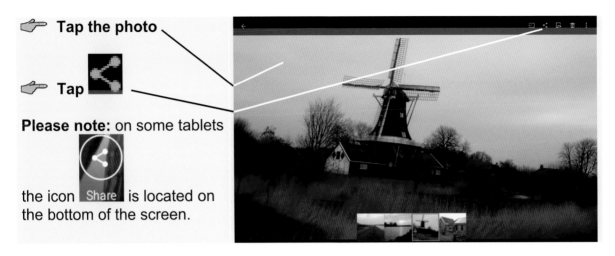

Please note: on some tablets

the icon `Share` is located on the bottom of the screen.

You will see a window:

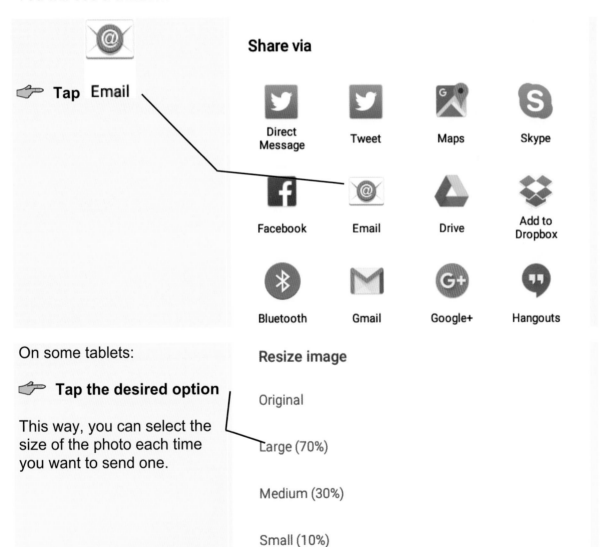

☞ **Tap Email**

Share via

Direct Message   Tweet   Maps   Skype

Facebook   Email   Drive   Add to Dropbox

Bluetooth   Gmail   Google+   Hangouts

On some tablets:

☞ **Tap the desired option**

This way, you can select the size of the photo each time you want to send one.

Resize image

Original

Large (70%)

Medium (30%)

Small (10%)

A new message is opened, to which the photo has been added as an attachment:

You can send the message in the same way you did in *Chapter 2 Using Email on Your Tablet.* For now this will not be necessary:

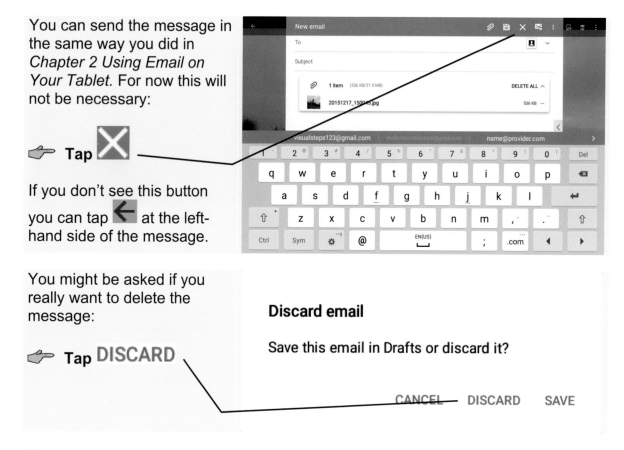

☞ **Tap** ✖

If you don't see this button you can tap ← at the left-hand side of the message.

You might be asked if you really want to delete the message:

☞ **Tap DISCARD**

Discard email

Save this email in Drafts or discard it?

CANCEL   DISCARD   SAVE

You will see the photo again.

7.5 Printing a Photo

If you have a wireless printer, you will probably be able to print through a wireless connection on your Samsung Galaxy Tab. You will need to make sure Wi-Fi is enabled. You also might need to download an app that goes with your printer. Not all printers will support this function, but if yours does, you start like this:

☞ **If necessary, tap the photo**

☞ **Tap** ⁝

☞ **Tap Print**

On some tablets you need to tap the **Share** icon at the bottom of the screen:

At the bottom of the screen:

☞ **Tap** Share

A menu appears:

☞ **Tap** Print

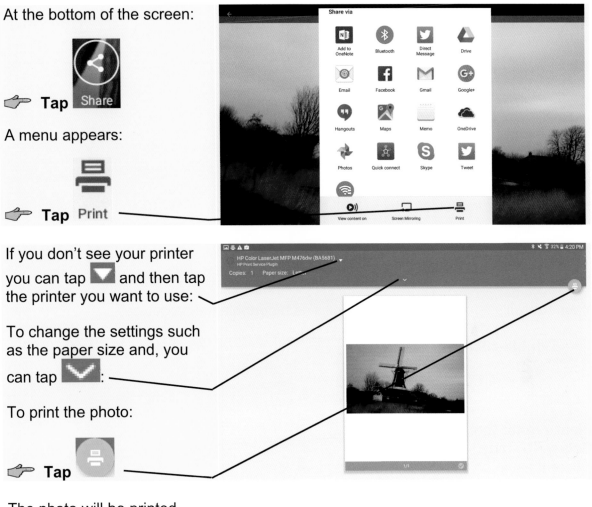

If you don't see your printer you can tap ⬇ and then tap the printer you want to use:

To change the settings such as the paper size and, you can tap ⌄ :

To print the photo:

☞ **Tap**

The photo will be printed.

☞ **Go back to the home screen** ³

7.6 Copying Photos and Videos to the Computer

You can copy the photos and videos you have made with your Samsung Galaxy Tab to your computer with *File Explorer*. You do that like this:

☞ **Connect the Samsung Galaxy Tab to the computer**

☞ **If necessary, close the *AutoPlay* window** ⁷

Open *File Explorer* on the Taskbar, on your desktop:

⊕ **Click**

In *Windows 8.1* the folder *This PC* will be opened. *In Windows 10* and *7* you will need to open it first:

⊕ **Click** 🖥 Computer **or** 🖥 This PC

Your Tab will be recognized by *Windows* as a portable media device:

⊕ **Double-click**

Studio Visual Ste (SM-

Please note: your Samsung Galaxy Tab may have a different name on your own computer.

⊕ **Double-click**

Tablet
10.6 GB free of 11.9 GB

The photos and videos are stored in a folder called *DCIM*:

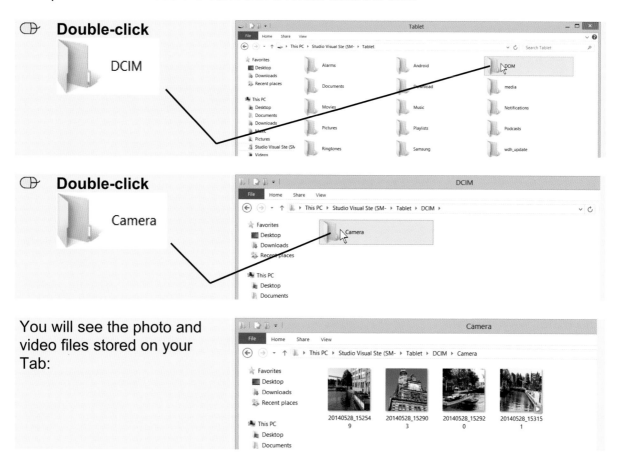

Double-click DCIM

Double-click Camera

You will see the photo and video files stored on your Tab:

This is how you copy these photos to the (*My*) *Pictures* folder on your computer, for example:

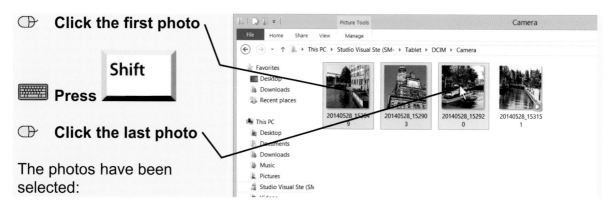

Click the first photo

Press Shift

Click the last photo

The photos have been selected:

When you drag the photos to a folder on your computer, they will be copied:

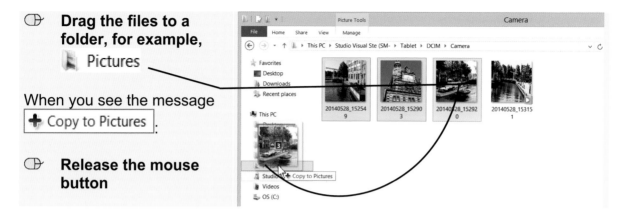

⊕ **Drag the files to a folder, for example,** Pictures

When you see the message .

⊕ **Release the mouse button**

Now the pictures have been copied to your computer. You can use the same method to copy a video to your computer.

♀ **Tip**
The other way round
This also works if you want to copy photos and videos from your computer to your

Samsung Galaxy Tab. It is better to put the photos you copy in the ▦ Pictures folder. Then they will be displayed in a separate album.

🖝 **Close** *File Explorer* 👣7

🖝 **Disconnect the Samsung Galaxy Tab from the computer**

7.7 Play a Recorded Video

In *section 7.2 Filming* you recorded a short video. You can watch this video with the *Video* app:

☞ **If necessary, tap** ▦

☞ **Tap** Video

You will see the thumbnail image of the video(s) you have recorded:

☞ **Tap the video**

The video will be played right away:

If you tap the screen, you will see the playback options:

You can use the slider to rewind or go fast forward: ———

You will see a Pause playback button: ———

☞ **Go back to the home screen** 👣³

☞ **Lock or turn off the Samsung Galaxy Tab, if you wish** 👣⁸

In this chapter you have become acquainted with the *Camera, Gallery*, and *Video* apps.

7.8 Background Information

Dictionary

Album	The name of the folder that contains the photos you have taken with your Samsung Galaxy Tab, or the ones that have been stored on your Samsung Galaxy Tab, for example, by saving an attachment or saving a photo from a website.
Camera	An app with which you can take pictures and record videos. You can use both the front and rear cameras on the Samsung Galaxy Tab for this.
Gallery	An app that lets you view your photos on the Samsung Galaxy Tab.
Slideshow	An automatic display of a collection of images.
Video	An app with which you can watch the videos on your Samsung Galaxy Tab.
Zoom in	Take a closer look.
Zoom out	View from further away.

Source: User manual Samsung Galaxy Tab, Wikipedia

7.9 Tips

 Tip

Use a photo as a background
You can also use your own photo as a background image for the lock screen or the home screen. You do that like this:

☞ **If necessary, tap the photo** ──────────

☞ **Tap ⦙ or** MORE ──────

☞ **If necessary, drag upwards over the menu**

☞ **Tap** Set as **or** Set as wallpaper ──────

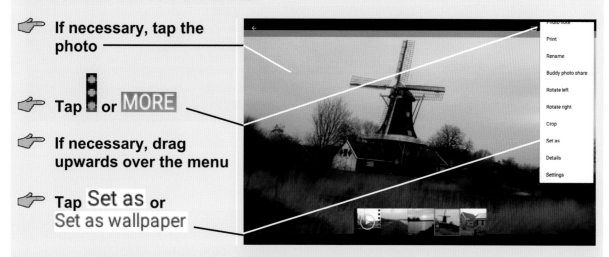

If you want to set this photo as a background picture for the home screen:

☞ **Tap** Home screen ──────

On some tablets you will see this message:

☞ **If necessary, tap** Crop picture ──────

☞ **If necessary, tap** JUST ONCE ──────

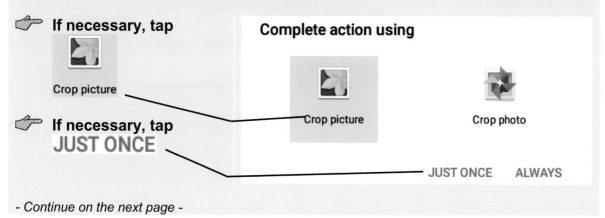

- Continue on the next page -

On some tablets you can select which part of the picture you want to use:

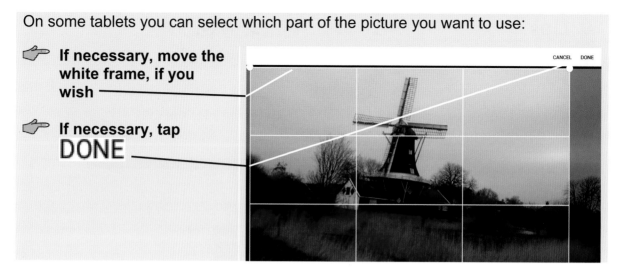

👉 **If necessary, move the white frame, if you wish** ——

👉 **If necessary, tap DONE** ——

💡 **Tip**

Photo editing

On some tablets you can use simple photo editing tools in the *Gallery* app. For instance, rotating or cropping a photo, adjusting the color and exposure, and adding some effects. This is not available as default on some tablets. In the *Galaxy Apps store* you can download various free and paid photo editing apps.

👉 **Open the *Gallery* app** **21**

👉 **Tap a photo**

👉 **Tap**  **or** **Edit**

When *Photo Editor* isn't installed yet, you will see this message:

👉 **Tap DOWNLOAD** ——

You might see a message about terms and conditions:

👉 **Tap AGREE**

- Continue on the next page -

The *Galaxy Apps store* will be opened:

☞ **Tap** INSTALL

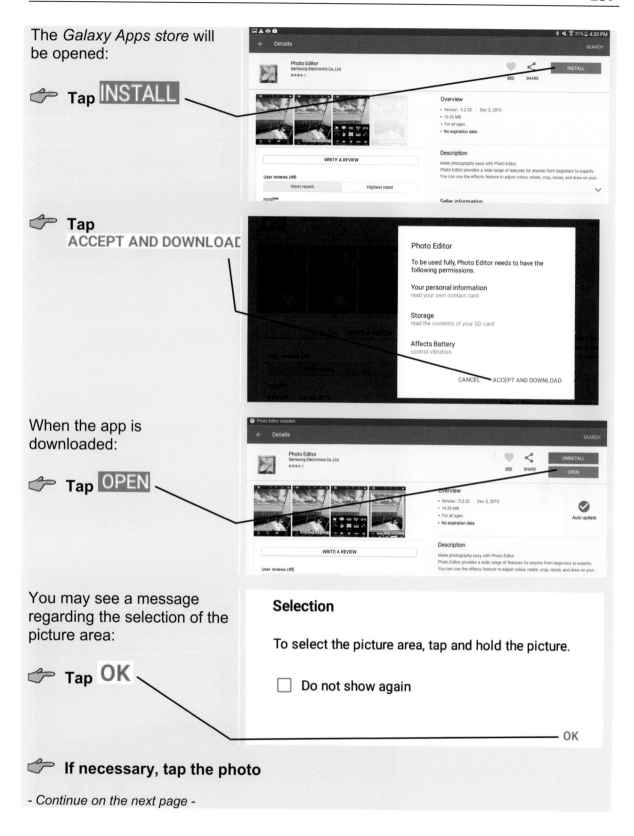

☞ **Tap**
ACCEPT AND DOWNLOAD

When the app is downloaded:

☞ **Tap** OPEN

You may see a message regarding the selection of the picture area:

☞ **Tap** OK

☞ **If necessary, tap the photo**

- Continue on the next page -

Below the photo you will see several options. You can give some of these options a try:

 Rotate rotate a photo.

 Crop crop a photo.

 Color adjust the color.

 Effect add an effect.

 Sticker add a sticker.

 Drawing draw on the photo.

 Frames add a frame.

You can undo any changes with ⤺ or UNDO:

Use **Save** to save the edited photo. The photo will be saved in the *Camera* album or in a new album in the *Gallery* app. The original photo will be saved as well.

Tip

Transfer photos from a memory card to the Tab

If you have a Micro SD card with photos, for example, you can transfer them to your Tab like this:

☞ **Insert the SD card into the memory card slot**

☞ **Open the *My Files* app** ⚙️27

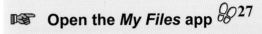 👉 **Tap** **SD card**

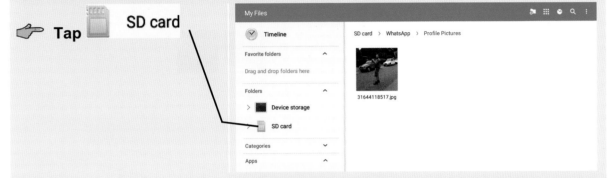

👉 **Tap** **DCIM**

👉 **Tap** **Camera**

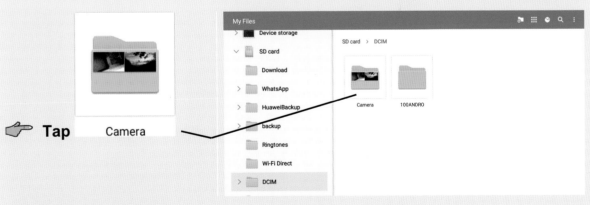

- Continue on the next page -

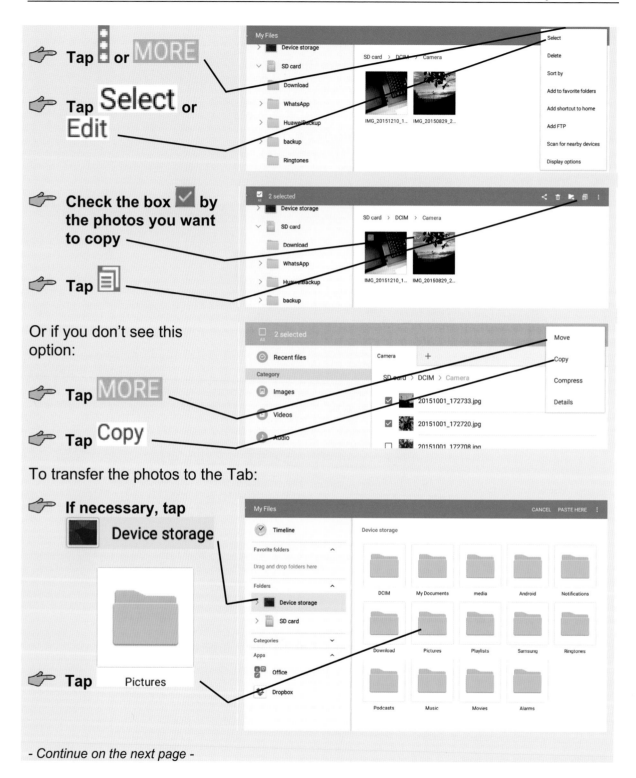

☞ Tap ⋮ or MORE

☞ Tap Select or Edit

☞ Check the box ✅ by the photos you want to copy

☞ Tap 🗐

Or if you don't see this option:

☞ Tap MORE

☞ Tap Copy

To transfer the photos to the Tab:

☞ If necessary, tap ▪ Device storage

☞ Tap Pictures

- Continue on the next page -

You will see the files that have already been placed in the folder:

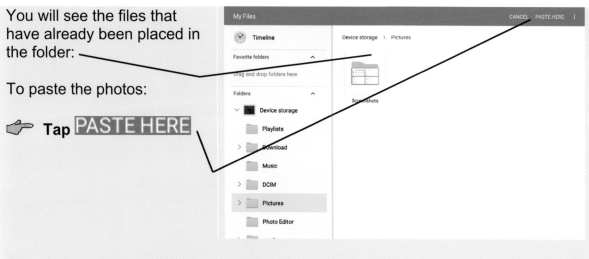

To paste the photos:

☞ Tap PASTE HERE

The photos will be copied to your Tab.

Tip

Upload a video to YouTube
You can upload a video directly to *YouTube* from within the *Video* app. To do that:

☞ **Open the *Video* app** ᕀ**22**

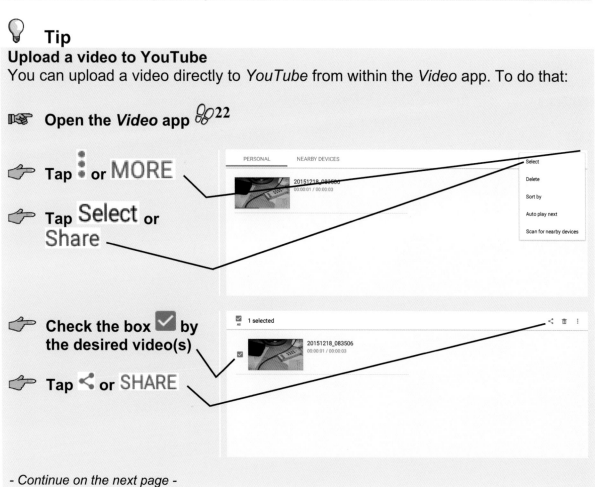

☞ **Tap ⋮ or MORE**

☞ **Tap Select or Share**

☞ **Check the box ☑ by the desired video(s)**

☞ **Tap < or SHARE**

- Continue on the next page -

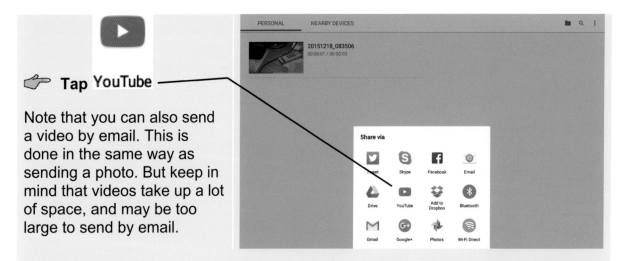

☞ **Tap** YouTube

Note that you can also send a video by email. This is done in the same way as sending a photo. But keep in mind that videos take up a lot of space, and may be too large to send by email.

In order to upload the video to *YouTube* you will need to sign in with your *Google* account. Next, you can enter the information for the video on the screen.

Tip!
YouTube also has its own app. This app is installed on your Tab by default. With this app you can easily watch all sorts of movies on *YouTube*. You can also create playlists with your favorite films, for example.

8. Music

Your Samsung Galaxy Tab comes with an extensive music player called the *Music* app. If you have music files stored on your computer, you can copy these files to your Samsung Galaxy Tab with *File Explorer*.

In this chapter you will learn how to:

- copy music to your Samsung Galaxy Tab;
- play music on your Samsung Galaxy Tab;
- create a playlist on your Samsung Galaxy Tab;
- delete music from your Samsung Galaxy Tab.

 Please note:

While you are using your Tab, you may see some screens that provide additional information about the operation of an app or the keyboard. You can read the information and tap DONE or OK afterwards.

8.1 Copying Music to Your Samsung Galaxy Tab

Once the songs (also called tracks) are displayed in *File Explorer*, it is very easy to add them to your Tab.

☞ **Connect your Samsung Galaxy Tab to the computer**

☞ **If necessary, close the help window** ℘⁷

☞ **Open *File Explorer*** ℘³⁴

The Samsung Galaxy Tab will appear in *File Explorer*. First you select the tracks you want to copy. In this example the tracks are located in the *Music* folder:

By 🖥 **This PC or** 🖥 **Computer, click** >

Click 🎵 **Music**

You will see the files in the *Music* folder:

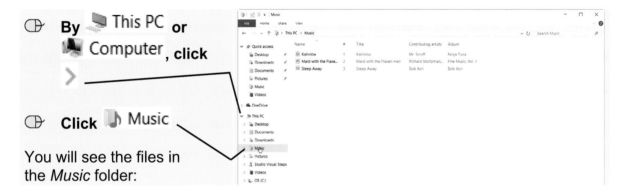

You are going to select the tracks:

Click the first track

Press [Shift] **and hold it down**

Click the third track

Release [Shift]

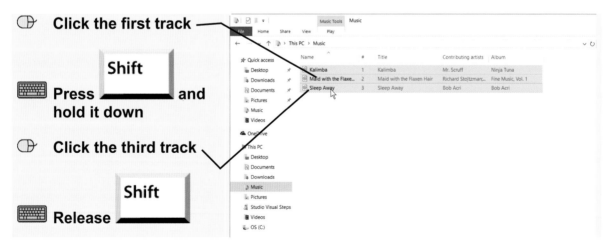

The tracks have been selected. Now you can copy them to your Samsung Galaxy Tab:

Right-click the selected tracks

You will see a menu:

Click Copy

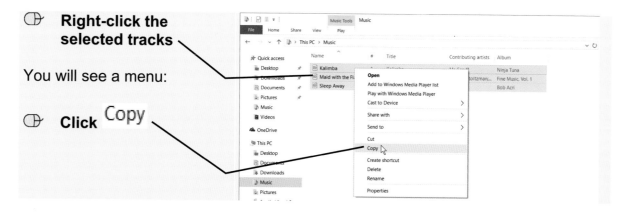

Now you can open the *Music* folder on your tablet. First you need to open the tablet:

The tablet is shown at the left-hand side of the window:

Click your tablet

Double-click Tablet

Double-click Music

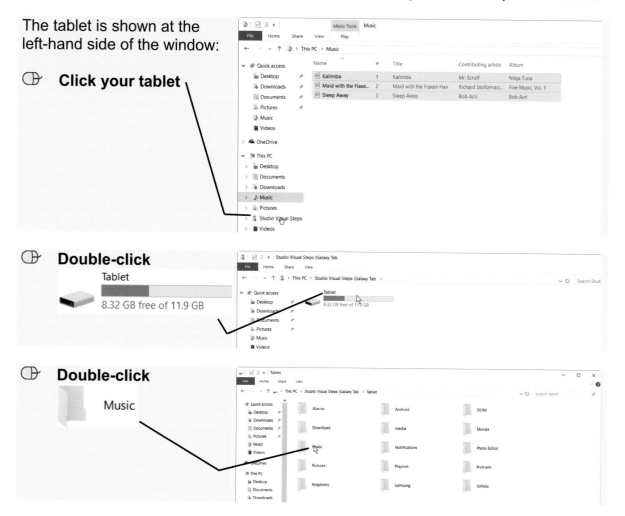

⊙ **Right-click an empty spot in the right pane**

You will see a menu:

⊙ **Click** Paste

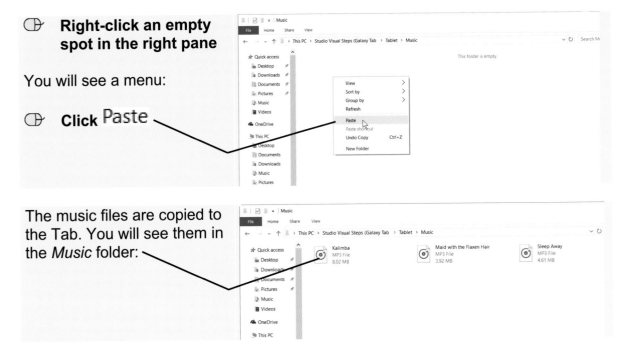

The music files are copied to the Tab. You will see them in the *Music* folder:

Now you can disconnect the Tab:

☞ **Disconnect the Samsung Galaxy Tab**

In the *Tips* at the end of this chapter you can read how to delete tracks from the Tab and how to create a playlist.

8.2 Playing Music

You can also use the *Music* app to play your music. To open the app:

☞ **If necessary, tap** ▦

☞ **Tap** Music

👉 **Tap** TRACKS

👉 **Tap a title, for example**

Sleep Away

Bob Acri / Bob Acri

👉 **Tap the cover of the album**

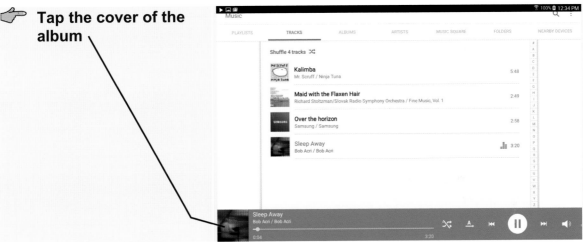

The music player is displayed much larger:

You will see various buttons that can be used to control how the music is played:

Here is what these control buttons do:

 Mutes the volume.

 This button has multiple functions:
- tap once: go to the next song.
- press your finger on the button to fast forward.

 This button has multiple functions:
- tap once: go to the beginning of the current song.
- tap twice: go to the previous song.
- press your finger on the button to rewind.

 Pause play.

 Resume play.

 Drag the play button or tap the bar to go to a specific part of the song.

 Randomly play a song.

 The songs will not be repeated.

Repeat:

- tap once: all songs will be repeated. The button turns into [A].
- tap twice: the current song is repeated. The button turns into [1].

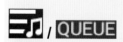 On the left-hand side of the screen you will see a pane with a list of all the tracks.

 Add a song to the favorite tracks. Not available on all tablets.

If you click 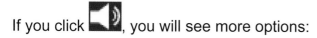, you will see more options:

	Volume control.
	Select a sound effect. Not available on all tablets.

While playing a song, you can leave the *Music* app and do something else:

☞ **Go back to the home screen** 👣3

The music is still playing. You can display the control buttons of the *Music* app in the *Notification Panel* any time when using another app:

☞ **Open the *Notification Panel*** 👣1

You will see the volume control buttons of the *Music* app. To pause the music:

☞ **Tap** ⏸

☞ **Tap** ✕

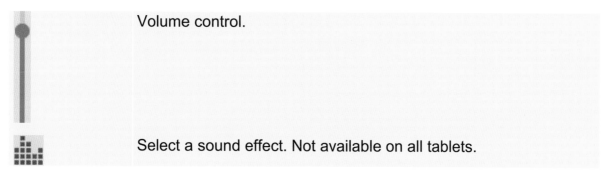

☞ **Go back to the home screen** 👣3

☞ **Lock or turn off the Samsung Galaxy Tab, if you wish** 👣8

You have nearly reached the end of this book. In this book you have learned how to work with the Samsung Galaxy Tab. Now you can start exploring some more and discover additional options and features this handy device has to offer.

8.4 Visual Steps Website and Newsletter

By now we hope you have noticed that the Visual Steps method is an excellent method for quickly and efficiently learning more about computers, tablets, other devices and software applications. All books published by Visual Steps use this same method.
In various series, we have published a large number of books on a wide variety of topics including *Windows*, *Mac OS X*, the iPad, iPhone, Samsung Galaxy Tab, Kindle, photo editing and many other topics.

On the **www.visualsteps.com** website you will find a full product summary by clicking the blue *Catalog* button. For each book there is an extensive description, the full table of contents and a sample chapter (PDF file). In this way, you can quickly determine if a specific title will meet your expectations. You can order a book directly online from this website or other online book retailers. All titles are also available in bookstores in the USA, Canada, United Kingdom, Australia and New Zealand.

Furthermore, the website offers many extras, among other things:
- free computer guides and booklets (PDF files) covering all sorts of subjects;
- frequently asked questions and their answers;
- information on the free Computer Certificate that you can acquire at the certificate's website **www.ccforseniors.com**;
- a free email notification service: let's you know when a new book is published.

There is always more to learn. Visual Steps offers many other books on computer-related subjects. Each Visual Steps book has been written using the same step-by-step method with short, concise instructions and screen shots illustrating every step.

Would you like to be informed when a new Visual Steps title becomes available? Subscribe to the free Visual Steps newsletter (no strings attached) and you will receive this information in your inbox.
The Newsletter is sent approximately each month and includes information about
- the latest titles;
- supplemental information concerning titles previously released;
- new free computer booklets and guides;
When you subscribe to our Newsletter you will have direct access to the free booklets on the **www.visualsteps.com/info_downloads.php** web page.

8.4 Background Information

Dictionary

Music	An app with which you can play music.
Playlist	A collection of songs, arranged in a certain order.

Source: User manual Samsung Galaxy Tab

8.5 Tips

 Tip
Create a playlist
One of the nice features in the *Music* app is the ability to create your own playlist. In a playlist, you collect your favorite songs and arrange them in the order you wish. Once you have done this, you can play the playlist over and over again. Here is how to create a new playlist in the *Music* app.

In the top left-hand corner of the screen:

☞ **Tap** PLAYLISTS

☞ **Tap** +

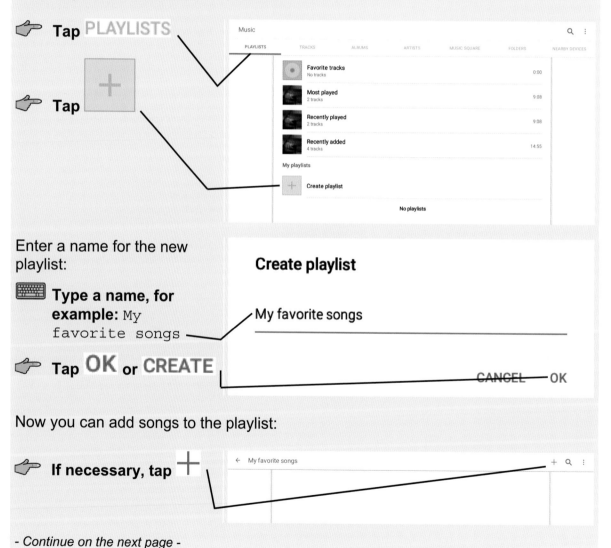

Enter a name for the new playlist:

⌨ **Type a name, for example:** My favorite songs

☞ **Tap** OK **or** CREATE

Now you can add songs to the playlist:

☞ **If necessary, tap** +

- Continue on the next page -

👉 **Tap the checkbox** ✅
   by the desired songs

To remove a song from the
playlist you can tap the

checkmark ✅ by the desired
song to uncheck the box.

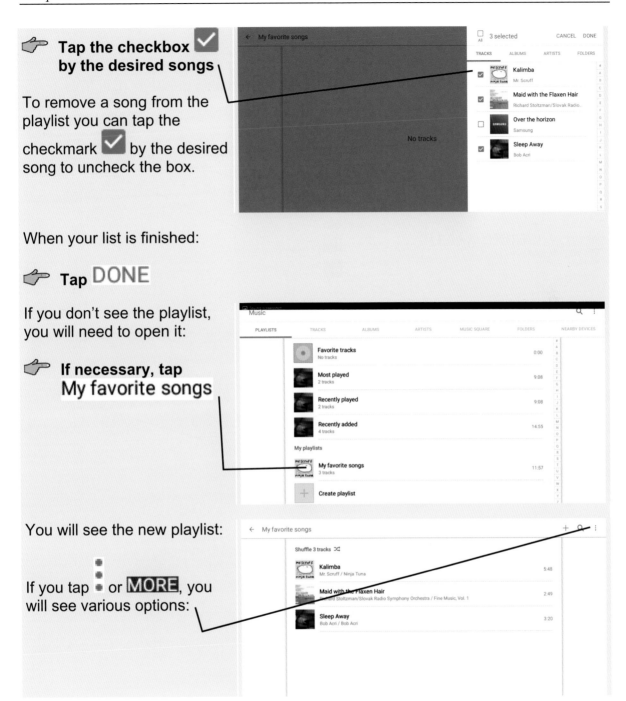

When your list is finished:

👉 **Tap** DONE

If you don't see the playlist,
you will need to open it:

👉 **If necessary, tap**
   My favorite songs

You will see the new playlist:

If you tap ⋮ or **MORE**, you
will see various options:

� Tip

Delete a track from the Samsung Galaxy Tab

In the *Music* app on your Samsung Galaxy Tab you can also delete songs. This is how you delete a song:

☞ Tap TRACKS

☞ Tap ⋮ or MORE

☞ Tap Delete or Edit

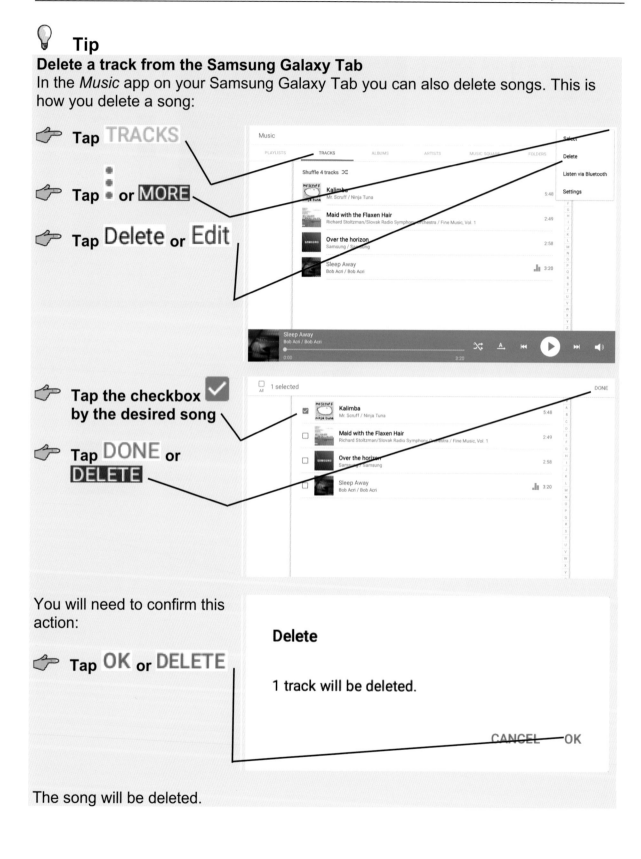

☞ Tap the checkbox ✔
by the desired song

☞ Tap DONE or
DELETE

You will need to confirm this action:

☞ Tap OK or DELETE

Delete

1 track will be deleted.

CANCEL   OK

The song will be deleted.

Appendices

A. How Do I Do That Again?

The actions and exercises in this book are marked with footsteps:

If you have forgotten how to do something, you can read how to do it again by finding the corresponding number in the list below.

1 Open *Notification Panel*
- Drag your finger downwards, starting at the top of the screen

2 Display the status bar
- Drag your finger downwards, starting at the top of the screen

3 Go back to the home screen
- Press the Home button

4 Turn on the Tab
- Press and hold the Power/Lock button ⓪ ( ) until the you see the Samsung logo

5 Open the *Settings* app
- Open the *Notification Panel* 1
- Tap ⚙

6 Open a website on the computer
In Windows 10 or 8.1:
- On the Taskbar, click 🅴 or

In Windows 7:
- Click 🪟
- Click ▶ All Programs
- Click 🅴 Internet Explorer

In all versions:
- Type the web address in the address bar
- Press **Enter**

7 Close a window
- Click ✕ or ✕

8 Lock or turn off the Tab
- Press the Power/Lock button ⓪ ( )

Completely turn off:
- Press and hold the Power/Lock button ⓪ ( ) for a few seconds
- Tap ⏻ Power off
- Tap POWER OFF

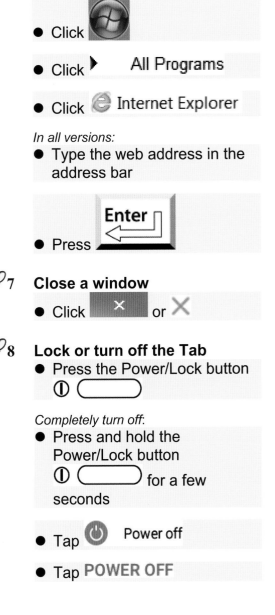

🦶9 Unlock the Tab
- Press the Power/Lock button
  ⏻ ⬭
- Drag across the screen

🦶10 Open a new memo
- Tap ▦

- Tap Memo

- If necessary, tap ⊕

🦶11 Open *Smart Switch* on the computer
In Windows 10 on Taskbar on the desktop:
- Click the search bar

In Windows 10 on the desktop and in Windows 8.1, from the Start screen:
- Type: Smart Switch

- Click Ⓢ Smart Switch

In Windows 7:

- Click ⊞

- Click ▶ All Programs

- Click Samsung

- Click Smart Switch PC

- Click Ⓢ Smart Switch

🦶12 Open the *Email* app
- Tap ▦

- Tap Email

🦶13 Open an email
- If necessary, tap

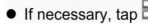 Inbox

- Tap the message

🦶14 Go to another tab
- Tap the desired tab

🦶15 Take a picture
- If necessary, tap ▦

- Tap Camera

- Tap ◉

🦶16 Add a contact
- Tap ➕

- Tap ▼

- Tap a field

- Type the data

- Repeat this for all the fields you want to use

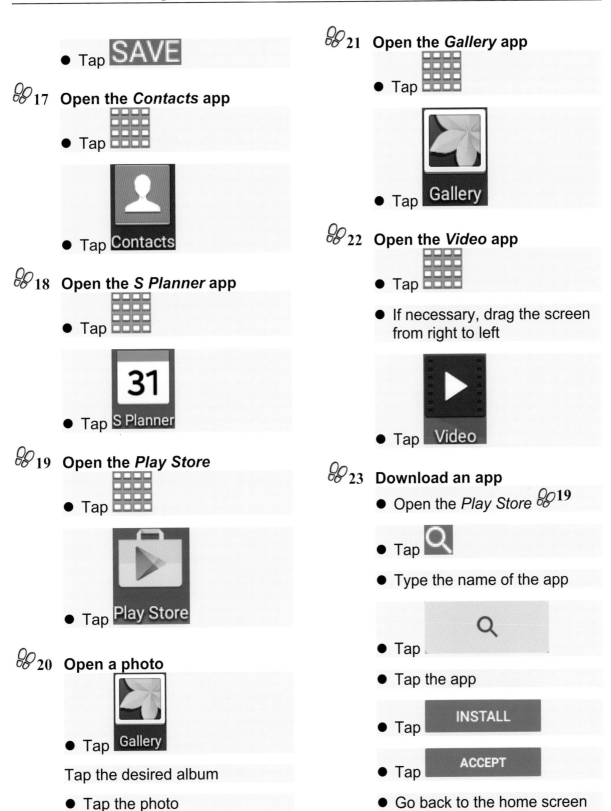

- Tap SAVE

17 Open the *Contacts* app

- Tap [grid icon]

- Tap Contacts

18 Open the *S Planner* app

- Tap [grid icon]

- Tap S Planner

19 Open the *Play Store*

- Tap [grid icon]

- Tap Play Store

20 Open a photo

- Tap Gallery

Tap the desired album

- Tap the photo

21 Open the *Gallery* app

- Tap [grid icon]

- Tap Gallery

22 Open the *Video* app

- Tap [grid icon]

- If necessary, drag the screen from right to left

- Tap Video

23 Download an app

- Open the *Play Store* 𝖌𝖌19

- Tap [search icon]

- Type the name of the app

- Tap [search field]

- Tap the app

- Tap INSTALL

- Tap ACCEPT

- Go back to the home screen 𝖌𝖌3

24 Open the *Play Books* app

- Tap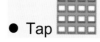

- Tap

25 Open the *Facebook or Twitter* app

- Tap

- If necessary, drag the screen from right to left

- Tap

26 Open the *Skype* app

- Tap

- If necessary, drag the screen from right to left

- Tap

27 Open the *My Files* app

- Tap

- Tap

28 Move an app

- Place your finger on the app you want to move

- Drag the app to the left or right edge of the screen

When you see the other page:
- Release the app

29 Delete text

- Tap to set the cursor at the end of the text (right side)

- Press  until the desired text has been deleted

30 Add a widget

- Press your finger to the Home screen

- Tap

- Place your finger on the widget

- Drag to the desired page and release the widget

31 Open the *Internet* app

- Tap

- Tap Internet

32 Open a website on the Tab
- Type the web address in the address bar

- Tap Go

33 Zoom in
- Double-tap an empty section of the web page

Or:
- Spread your thumb and index finger away from each other as you touch the screen

34 Open *File Explorer*
On the Taskbar, on your desktop:

- Click

B. Index

A

Accents typing	64
Account	78, 90
Add	
email account	78
new user	74
Adjusting selection	84
Adjusting view calendar	137
Airplane mode	28, 59
Alarm	179
Album	236
Android	59
Antivirus app	213
App(s)	26, 59, 205
closing	173
deleting	203
downloading	186
list	178
managing	196
moving	197
purchased app	190
searching in *Play Store*	191
storing in folder	199
switching between apps	117
updating	206
App icons	59
Attachment	98
send	99
Automatically updating Tab	39

B

Back button	24, 25, 59
Backup	
creating	69
restoring	71
Basic operations	29
BCC	82
Bluetooth	28, 59

Bookmark	121
adding	113
deleting	122
opening	114
Books downloading	182

C

Calculator	179
Calendar	
adjusting view	137
keeping	136
synchronising with *Outlook*	155
Calendar (see *S Planner*)	
Camera	219, 220, 236
filming	222
taking photo(s)	220
Capital letters typing	36
CC	82
Changing keyboard view	37, 38
Changing label	130
Checking for updates in *Play Store*	206
Chrome	179
Closing	
apps	173
tab in app *Internet*	111
Comma typing	35
Components Tab	24
Connecting Tab to computer	49
Connecting to Internet	
through mobile data network	44
through Wi-Fi	41
Contact	
add	128
add field	131
add a photo	149
deleting	135
deleting field	151
editing	134
searching	135

synchronising 151
Contacts 82, 90, 127, 148
  opening 128
Copying 84
  music 246
  photo(s) to computer 232
  photo(s) to Tab 241
  video(s) to computer 232
Creating
  backup 69
  Google account 52
  playlist 254
  Samsung account 96
Cut 84

D

Data roaming 46, 61
Date and time setting up 21, 31
Deleting
  app 203
  bookmark 122
  contact 135
  directions 166
  downloaded file 172
  email 87
  event 140
  history 124
  music 256
  note 38
  photo 228
  text 84
  widget 147
Directions
  deleting 166
  getting 164
Disabling *Predictive text* 95
Disconnecting Tab safely 51
Download history 175
Downloading
  app 186, 190
  books 182
  file 169
  purchased app for second time 208

Smart Switch 47
Downloads 157
Drive 179
Dropbox 23, 59, 179

E

EDGE 28, 59
Email 77, 90
  opening 78
Email(ing)
  account 78
  deleting 87
  displaying folder list 87
  moving to another folder 92
  opening 85
  opening blank email 81
  photo 228
  receiving 85
  retrieving 86
  sending 81, 85
Event 148
  adding 137
  deleting 140
  editing 140
Exclamation mark typing 35

F

Facebook app 208
Fetch 90, 94
Field 131, 148, 151
  adding 131
  deleting 151
File downloading 169
File Explorer opening 232
Filming 222
Firmware 60, 72
  upgrading through *Smart Switch* 72

G

Gallery 219, 224, 236
  deleting photo(s) 228
  printing 230

sending photo(s) by email 228
slideshow 227
viewing photo(s) 224
Getting directions 164
Gmail 77, 90, 92
Google 121
+ 179
Calendar 148
Gift Card 185, 190, 205
Search 157
Settings 179
typing with voice control 65
Google account 22, 60, 205
creating/adding 52
GPRS 28, 60

H

Hancom viewer 179
Hangouts 148, 180
Help 180
History viewing and deleting 124
Home button 23, 24, 33, 60
Home page 121
setting 125
Home screen 23, 30, 60
Hyperlink 121

I

Icons status bar 26
IMAP (*Internet Message Acces Protocol*) 79
Inbox 85, 90
Incoming email 85
Inserting SIM card 45
Internet (app) 101
opening 102
Internet
connecting through mobile data network 44
connecting through Wi-Fi 41

K

Keyboard view 37, 38

L

Label 148
changing 130
Language setting up 19
Link 121
opening in a new tab 110
opening on a web page 109
List of apps 178
List of icons 27
Location
viewing with *Street View* 161
searching 161
Location services 22, 60
Lock screen 32, 60, 66
Locking 60
Tab 57
with pattern 66

M

Managing apps 196
Maps 157, 175
changing view 159
deleting directions 166
extensive information 176
getting directions 164
opening 158
searching location 161
Street View 161
Memo (see Notes)
Memo opening 34
Messaging 180
Micro SD card 60
Microsoft Exchange ActiveSync 79
Moving app 197
Multi window 118
Music (app) 245, 248, 253
Music
copying to Tab 246
deleting from Tab 256

playing   248
My Files   157, 169, 175

N

Note
  deleting   38
  saving   38
  taking   34
Notification Panel opening   30

O

Onscreen keyboard   34
Open attachment   98
Opening
  File Explorer   232
  Maps   158
  Memo   34
  Notification Panel   30
  Settings   30
  tab in app *Internet*   110, 112
Outlook   148, 151
  synchronising calendar   155
Outlook.com   90

P

Pasting a word   84
PayPal   185, 190, 205
Period   35
Phone   180
Photo(s)   180
  adding to a contact   149
  as background   237
  copying to computer   232
  editing   238
  emailing   228
  printing   230
  taking   220
  transferring from memory card   241
  viewing in *Gallery*   224
Play Books   180, 182
Play Games   180
Play Movies & TV   181

Play Music   181
Play Newsstand   181
Play Store   17, 61, 205
Playing
  music   248
  video   234
Playlist   253
  creating   254
  deleting track   255
POP (*Post Office Protocol*)   79
Power/Lock button   18, 61
Predictive text   82, 90
  accepting   83
  disabling   95
Printing photo   230
Push   90, 94

Q

Question mark   35
Quickly type web address   122

R

Recent apps button   24, 25, 61
Restoring backup   71
Retrieving email   86
Roaming (see Data roaming)
Rotate screen automatic   31

S

S Planner   127, 136, 148
S Voice   181
Safely disconnecting Tab   51
Samsung account   22, 61
  creating   96
Samsung Apps   181
Samsung Galaxy Tab (see Tab)
Samsung Go   181
Saving note   38
Scrolling   33, 107, 121
  sideways   107
Search   26, 167, 175
  settings   177

Searching
    app in *Play Store* — 191
    contact — 135
    in app *Internet* — 115
    location — 161
Selecting a word — 84
Selection adjusting — 84
Selfportrait — 221
Send attachment — 99
Sending email — 85
Setting up
    date and time — 21
    language — 19
    sounds — 63
    Tab — 19
Settings opening — 30
Shortcuts to apps — 26
SideSync — 181
Signature — 90
    adding — 91
SIM card — 44, 61
    inserting — 45
Simlock — 44, 61
Skype — 217
Slideshow — 236
Smart stay — 28, 61, 73
Smart Switch — 47, 61
    creating a backup — 69
    download — 47
    restoring a backup — 71
Sounds setting up — 63
Special symbols typing — 37
Status bar — 26
Stored pages — 121, 126
Storing for offline reading — 126
Street View — 161, 175
Switching
    between apps — 117
    cameras — 221
Symbols (see Icons)
Synchronizing — 61, 148
    calendar — 155
    contacts — 151

T

Tab — 17, 61
    automatically updating — 39
    basic operations — 29
    components — 24
    connecting to computer — 49
    deleting music — 256
    home screen — 23, 30
    locking/turning off — 57
    Notification Panel opening — 30
    onscreen keyboard — 34
    safely disconnecting — 51
    setting up — 19
    turning on — 18
    unlocking — 18, 29
Tab (in app *Internet*)
    closing — 111
    opening — 110, 112
Tablet — 17, 62
Taking note — 35
Text
    copy, cut, paste — 84
    deleting — 84
    selecting — 84
Timeout screen — 62, 63
Traffic information — 177
Transfer photos/videos to Tab — 241
Trash — 87, 90
Twitter app — 211
Typing — 35
    accents — 64
    capital letter — 35
    comma — 35
    exclamation mark — 35
    period — 35
    special symbols — 37
    question mark — 35
Turning off Tab — 57
Turning on Tab — 18

U

Unlocking Tab — 18, 29
Updating — 205

apps   206
   Tab   39
Uploading video to *YouTube*   243
Users   74
Using
   Facebook app   208
   Skype app   217
   Twitter app   211

V

Video (app)   181, 236
Video(s)
   copying to computer   232
   playing   234
   uploading to *YouTube*   243
View keyboard changing   37, 38
Viewing a location with *Street View* 161
Viewing history   124
Visual Steps website/newsletter   252
Voice Search   182

W

Web page
   adding bookmark   113
   opening   103

   to previous/next   112
Widget(s)   26, 62, 142
   deleting   147
   placing on page   145
   viewing   144
Wi-Fi   20, 41, 62
Word
   pasting   84
   selecting   84

Y

YouTube   182, 243

Z

Zooming in and out   104, 121, 226, 236

0

3G/4G (network)   28, 62

You and Your Windows 10 Computer

Are you taking full advantage of what a computer has to offer? Only if you really know what can be done with a computer and the Internet, will you be able to benefit from the fun and convenience it can give you.

This comprehensive book discuss many topics such as managing files, making useful settings, using email securely, working with Skype and social media services such as Facebook and Twitter. You will also get acquainted with photo and video editing and learn more about the safe use of the Internet and online shopping. But this is not all, there are plenty of other tips on offer in this user-friendly, step-by-step book. Get started right away and discover what is possible.

> *Everything you need to know about your computer, Internet, digital pictures and more*

Author: Studio Visual Steps
ISBN 978 90 5905 432 5
Book type: Paperback, full color
Nr of pages: 352 pages
Accompanying website:
www.visualsteps.com/your10computer

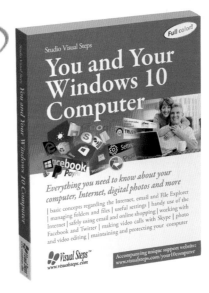

Learn how to:

- basic concepts regarding the Internet, email and File Explorer
- managing folders and files
- useful settings
- handy use of the Internet
- safely using email and online shopping
- working with Facebook and Twitter
- making video calls with Skype
- photo and video editing
- maintaining and protecting your computer

Suitable for:
Windows 10 on a desktop computer or laptop

Prior knowledge:
Basic knowledge of working with Windows

Creating a Website with WordPress

For many people today, creating and updating a personal website has become a fun and enjoyable hobby. A website can be used to share information about your family history, business, favorite genre of music or even to post the latest news and event information for a local club or organization. Thanks to a variety of software and online services, creating a website has never been easier. With the free,

> *For anyone who wants to create their own professional website*

user-friendly WordPress software, you can make your own personal and professional website in no time at all. This practical how-to book, shows you step by step exactly what to do. You start off by choosing an attractive theme (template) with which to build your website. Then you fill the website with your own text, pictures, videos and hyperlinks. You can even include a photo gallery, a pulldown menu with links to other pages, or an online form enabling people to contact you. These are just a few of the things that can be added to your website. WordPress offers a wide variety of plugins and widgets that can easily add extra functionality to your website. By using this book and the software from WordPress, you will have everything you need to create your own website!

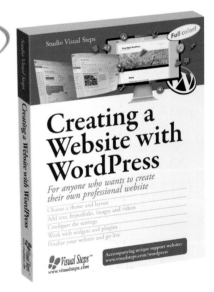

Author: Studio Visual Steps
ISBN 978 90 5905 422 6
Book type: Paperback, full color
Nr of pages: 264 pages
Accompanying website:
www.visualsteps.com/ wordpress

Learn how to:

- Choose a theme and layout
- Add text, hyperlinks, images and videos
- Configure the settings
- Work with widgets and plugins
- Finalize your website and go live

Suitable for:
Windows 10, 8.1, 7, Vista and Mac OS X